David Hummell Greer

Visions

Sunday Morning Sermons at St. Bartholomew's, New York

David Hummell Greer

Visions

Sunday Morning Sermons at St. Bartholomew's, New York

ISBN/EAN: 9783744755986

Printed in Europe, USA, Canada, Australia, Japan

Cover: Foto ©Lupo / pixelio.de

More available books at **www.hansebooks.com**

VISIONS

SUNDAY MORNING SERMONS AT ST. BARTHOLOMEW'S, NEW YORK

BY

DAVID H. GREER, D. D.
Rector of St. Bartholomew's Church, New York

NEW YORK
THOMAS WHITTAKER
2 AND 3 BIBLE HOUSE
1898

COPYRIGHT, 1898,
BY THOMAS WHITTAKER

PREFACE.

THE sermons in this volume were not delivered with any reference to the subsequent publication of them; and the only audience which the preacher had in mind when he preached them was the audience immediately before him. This will explain, if it does not excuse a redundancy and fragmentariness of style, which if not essential to direct discourse, are not incompatible with it, but which, in the preparation of an essay to be "harvested with the quiet eye" would naturally be avoided. This, however, is not a book of essays, but of sermons, or rather of the reports of sermons which were delivered originally without manuscript, and which are here printed, with a few verbal exceptions, precisely as they were preached. Some persons who heard them, and who thought that they were helped by them, have expressed the desire that they might be published, and that is why they are now put forth in this more permanent form.

CONTENTS.

	PAGE
Vision Through a Veil	9
Vision Through a Man	19
The Twilight Vision	31
The Vision of Mystery	43
The Vision of Doubt	53
Vision Books	67
The Christian Vision in Us	79
The Vision of the Divine Purpose	93
The Vision of the Divine Method; or, Bondage, Freedom and Obedience	105
The Self-revealing Vision	117
The Self-evidencing Visions	129
The Critical Vision, and the Loving Vision	141
The Vision of a Spiritual Guide	155
The Vision of Death	169
The Vision of Life	183
The Vision of Hell	195
The Vision of Heaven	207
The Vision of Good Making Evil	219
Visions in High Places	231
Visions in the Wilderness	243
The Vision of Social Unity	259
The Fulfilling Vision	273

VISION THROUGH A VEIL.

And the children of Israel saw the face of Moses, that the skin of Moses' face shone: and Moses put the veil upon his face.—EXODUS xxxiv. 35.

VISION THROUGH A VEIL.

Moses is here represented as having been on the mount in communion with God, and as having there received some vision of God, so exceptionally and transcendentally bright, that the face of Moses was transfigured by it. Then, when he came down from the mount to the people to give that vision to them, he is represented as putting a veil upon his face. And why? In order to conceal that vision? No, I think not, but in order to *reveal* it. That suggests the topic on which I wish to speak this morning—The Vision of God through a Veil.

There is no subject perhaps of physical inquiry more fascinatingly engaging, because so continually elusive, or which has received more attention upon the part of physical students, than the inquiry concerning *light*. Different theories about it, as you know, have been at times put forth. The latest theory, as you also know, and the one most generally and widely accepted, is this: That light is a wave of motion in the surrounding ether, whose velocity of undulation is so great that it produces the phenomenon of vision. But what is that wave of motion? Can we see it? We can *not* see it. And the curious thing about light, and the paradoxical thing, is this: That while it is the condition of all visibility, it is itself not visible, and can only be made to appear through the medium of other things on which it strikes or falls; on a bit of bamboo rod for instance—or a piece of glass, or a human face, or a marble column, a stone wall, a city, a world, a star, whether a burning star like the sun or a burnt out star like the moon—it can only I say be made to appear through the medium of something else. Light, in other words, is revealed when it is veiled. It is revealed through a veil, and only through a veil. Take away the veil, every veil, cities, houses, lands, waters, worlds, stars, every veil which, by resisting the light, makes it visible, then, while existing just the same, it is not visible.

That is the curious thing about light, yet the indisputably true thing, that it cannot be made to appear except by means of a veil.

What is true of the outer light is true of the inner light; true of the light of the mind, which we call "thought." We cannot see "thought" in itself. It is not in itself visible. How does it become visible? Only by coming into contact with, impinging upon, then struggling through, those little meshes of words in that marvelous veil of language, which so proverbially conceals as well as reveals; not letting the thought all out, in its spiritual entirety and nakedness, for then it would still be pure thought and invisible, but by offering some kind of impedimental resistance to it, hitting it, striking against it, and so, like the spark in the flint, making it shine and appear.

And the same is still more true of that more inward light, which we call the "light of the soul." We cannot see that light of the soul, for light cannot be seen. The condition of all visibility, it is itself invisible. How is it made to appear, that light of the soul? Through the veil, the fine, the beautiful veil of art, song, music, poetry, worship; or high, aspiring aim, reaching toward and struggling through some high ideal expression in conduct and in life. It cannot all get through. No man can wholly be what in his best and purest moods he wants to be. Something holds it back; yet by holding it back seems to let it out, seems to let it through. Sometimes it is a great joy that cannot be fully embodied, which it struggles through. Sometimes it is a great grief that cannot be fully disclosed, which it struggles through. Sometimes it is just the great sob or sigh of an inarticulate prayer, which it struggles through, in a groaning that cannot be uttered, holding it back, yet letting it out, as through the meshes of a veil, which conceals as well as reveals that spiritual light of the soul.

Now let us go on a little further. Physical light; mental light; spiritual light: God is Light. If that be true, what follows? This follows: That the only vision which we can have of God is a vision of God through a veil. Some of us it seems to me do not quite understand that. We do not take it in, and are disposed to think that the only way in which we can have a vision of God, clear and full and sure, is by taking away the veil, or drawing aside the veil. We are like those friends of the Greek artist, who, in coming to look at the picture which the artist had painted upon the canvas, asked him, you remember, to draw aside the curtain to let them see the picture, and to whom you remember the artist replied, "The curtain is the picture." That was all there was to see; the curtain. Yes, all there was to see, but not all there was. The curtain was more than a curtain. The curtain was a veil, revealing the artist who painted it, whose inner artist light, whose inner genius light, just because it was light, could not have been revealed in any other way. And the curtain was the picture, of the artist, or rather of that inner spiritual light which constituted the artist in his essential self, expressing, revealing, and giving to those who on the painted curtain looked, the vision of that light; and of which, if the curtain had been taken away, they would have had no vision, and could have had no vision.

Even so are we, in looking at and thinking about this wonderfully painted curtain of physical nature before us, sometimes moved to say, or wish, "O, that the curtain might be drawn aside a little, that we might see the picture, the wonderful picture of God." And the curtain *is* the picture, revealing God, giving the vision of God, who could not be revealed in any other way. For God is Light, and light cannot be seen in itself, it can only be seen through a veil; and God cannot be seen in Himself, He can only be seen through a veil. And that is what it seems to me this curtain, this great curtain of nature is, which in its infinite bigness through the telescope we see, which in its infinite littleness through the microscope we see; that is what it seems to me this curtain of nature is; not a curtain only, it is a curtain that is more than a curtain; it is a curtain that is a veil, the veil of God, coming to us as Moses came down from the mount with the veil upon his face.

Doesn't it look like it? Think a moment. Secreting yet disclosing, just as a veil does. Concealing yet revealing, just as a veil does. Holding back the light, and resisting it; letting out the light, and liberating it; the light of wisdom, of power, of beneficence, of love, of goodness, of GOD; not without some little shading in it, screening it, and hiding it, yet letting out that light, of goodness, and of God; letting it out, through a veil!

Is there any other word which so finely and fitly describes what physical nature is?

But physical nature is not the only veil of God. Human nature is a veil of God; finer, thinner, more attenuated, of more delicate fibre than physical nature, revealing God more clearly, more fully; giving to us in many ways not a larger vision of God, but a better vision of God; in whose human powers, the heart, the conscience, the sovereignty of the will, the freedom of the spirit, the majesty of the mind, the indissoluble integrity of the personality; in whose human powers exercised so nobly, so beneficently, upon the earth at times, the light of God appears.

Have we not seen it, my friends, shining through the story of human life, with its heroisms, not only on the battlefield, but in the daily round of the household and the home, in its sufferings, in its chivalries, in its sacrificings of self in behalf of some great cause, principle or truth, "daring the right, and disregarding alike the Yea and Nay of the world"? In its human loves, stretching out its human hands to heal, to help, to bless, with its holy benedictions, the family and the nation; in the mother, the soldier, the patriot, the apostle, the martyr, the prophet? What does it all mean? What does it all seem to be, but the light of God struggling through the veil, this "veil of human flesh" as Saint Paul calls it, so aptly and so well? Holding back the light, yet letting out the light, as through the meshes of a veil, and causing it to appear.

But if this human veil has some fineness of texture in it, it also has some grossness of texture in it, thick, hard, coarse, darkened, by passion and sin, baseness, vileness, meanness; cruelties, wrongs, lusts of the flesh and of the eye, through which the light of God cannot so brightly shine; yet even at times shining a little through all that, like a diamond in the dirt. Once, however, and only once, in the best judgment of the civilized world, there appeared a form without grossness, without blemish, without sin, with a fineness of texture so fine, so purely and spiritually fine, that it seemed to have been fitted and made in some purely spiritual way, to be the veil of God, so responsive to God, that there we see, as nowhere else, the vision of Himself —God coming to us in Jesus Christ with the veil upon His face.

O, men and women, searching for God, and crying out at times and saying, "O, that we knew where we might find Him!" God is Light; therefore, He can only be revealed through a veil, and in Jesus Christ most brightly, most clearly is that veil of God. The love that shone in Jesus Christ, it was the love of God. The glory which appeared in Jesus Christ, it was the glory of God; Light of light, God of God, very God of very God, coming to us as Moses came down from the mount, with the veil upon his face!

VISION THROUGH A MAN.

I see the heavens opened, and the Son of man standing on the right hand of God.—THE ACTS vii. 56.

VISION THROUGH A MAN.

That was the vision which Saint Stephen saw, the vision of heaven and God through the medium of a man, opening heaven, near to God, very near, representing God, His power, His authority, His sovereignty, His right hand. That was the vision which he saw; and the question of how he saw it, whether objectively or subjectively, physically or spiritually, with his eyes or with his soul, while interesting, of course, is not to us important. That is not our question. Our question is—Do we see it, that vision of a man, opening heaven, revealing God; do we see it? Let us inquire.

First, let me speak of the need to-day of some such vision as that. Man is a born discoverer—so at least it seems—with the instinct always in him to discover something new. Down to the present time in the history of the world, or up to the present time, whichever way we put it, that instinct of discovery in him has had a fairly sufficing use and exercise in the attempted discovery of the world itself, as the house in which he dwells. That discovery now, however, has been almost completed; and with the exception of a few untenanted and perhaps untenantable rooms, at the extreme northern end of the house and the extreme southern end, and which we designate as the "Poles" of the house, there is nothing much left to discover of this territorial house, this geographical world. It has been pretty much all discovered and opened up; and not only been discovered, but also now, as never before, it has been possessed, occupied, moved into. And civilized man is now established in his big, cosmic dwelling-house, with a very complete and comfortable kind of establishment in it.

And now, having done all this, having discovered now the world, and pretty well opened it up, as the house in which he dwells; and having, too, to a great extent, taken possession of it—having done and discovered all this, what will he try to discover next? What is there left to discover? What is there left to do? What will he try to do? Will he simply go on trying to live, in his big dwelling-house, pretty much in the same way in which he is living in it now, with a few more cosmic conveniences and contrivances and adornments in it, which are not so different after all from those he has already, nor producing in it either a different type of life? That hardly seems enough. It is not enough, to gratify, to satisfy, what every man on earth seems born to be, and do. He is a born searcher, discoverer, with the instinct in him to try to find something strange and new; and unless, having discovered and opened up the world in which he is living now, he can somehow discover and open up to some extent some other kind of world, he will not be contented in the world in which he is living now.

So, as a matter of fact, to-day, we often see and find him, not contented in the world. Why? Because he does not have it? No; but because he *does* have it: and because that is all he has, and that is all he sees, the world; and the world to-day is getting a little old to him, and faded and wrinkled and commonplace, and he wants a new and different world; crying for it, like the child for the moon, and not to be appeased because he does not have it and nobody will give it to him!

We hear a great deal said to-day about the discontentedness of the people who do not have much in this world, and of how that discontentedness, associated as it so often is, with a deep and growing sense on their part of injury and wrong, is becoming formidable and threatening to the stability of our modern society. Ah, if they only knew of that other discontentedness, deeper, greater, so much more bitter, so much more embittering, drying up or poisoning the very springs of life, of those other people who *do* have much in this world, and who do not have anything else! what a surprising revelation it would be to them, as perhaps some day it will be, when they are where the people are whom now so much they envy and are so jealous of. Then they too will find when they have succeeded in opening up fairly well the world in which they are living now, that they will be as much as now, or more than now, discontented in it, unless they can go on and try at least some other world to open up and find.

That is what so many, in so many ways are trying now to do. In academic and philosophical ways, in radical and conservative ways, in biological ways, "turning the gaze within," looking into man and all that bears on man; looking into man, the discoverer of the world, and trying to discover the discoverer himself, hoping thus to find in the discoverer himself some new kind of world.

Then again in other ways, are they trying to do it, not so academic and philosophical, but queer, strange, bizarre; in all those Christian Sciences, faith cures, Telepathies, Theosophies, Esoteric Buddhisms, and other subtle occultisms, with whose nomenclature I am not familiar, but which seem to be cropping up and cropping out all around to-day. There may be something in them, something good and true—I do not know whether there is or not. There is usually something good in everything. But what to me they chiefly mean, or chiefly show, is this: that the vision which men have to-day of this present world, so clear, so bright, so full, is not enough. Some other vision they must have, of some other world, and that vision of some other world, in all these strange and novel ways they are trying to-day to find, and thinking perhaps that they do.

Then again, what is the significance of that growing interest in religion which, in spite of its worldliness—yes, *because* of its worldliness, is coming to be one of the symptomatic features of our time; which shows itself not only in controversies and discussions, about creeds and doctrines and the different books of the Bible, and what they mean and are, but also in a growing disposition upon the part of many to-day, after they have become fairly well off in the world, seeing it, having it, or a good part of it, to become themselves religious—not much perhaps, but a little. Yet why even the little? We know the motive which is so often attributed to them. "A little religion," it is said, "is quite a respectable thing. A little religion is quite a fashionable thing." When such persons put on a little religion, by going to some Church, taking a pew in some Church, which is said to be fashionable they can thus maintain, it is said, by means of such little religion, a more respectable look and appearance, and standing in the world. I do not believe it! It may be the case, to some extent, with some; yet even in their case there is another and deeper motive in them, so deep perhaps that they are not conscious of it; nevertheless it is in them. To some extent, and in some way, people must be religious to-day. They must be, or they will die! They cannot get on without it. The very fact of their worldly life, seeing it, and having it so much, will be their death! "A lamp's death, when replete with oil, it chokes. A stomach's death, when surcharged with food, it starves. The lamp, o'erswims with oil; the stomach flags, loaded with nurture;" and the man surcharged with the world, and nothing else, "that man's soul dies!" And people must be religious, a little, to keep themselves alive.

So in these various ways, and many more besides, we are made to see, that what so much we need to-day and are trying so hard to find, is something like that vision of another world, of an open heaven which Saint Stephen saw. Can we then that vision have, that vision see to-day? I think we can. And how? In the same manner precisely in which Saint Stephen saw it. How did he see it? How was he made to see it? Not by a labored argument; not by a discussion, curious or critical or philosophical; not by evidences or proofs, or what we usually call evidences or proofs. Through the medium of a *man* he was made to see it, opening heaven, another world, revealing to him God!

Can we not understand it? Have we not ourselves at times had such a vision as that, in such a way as that—through a man, an acquaintance perhaps, a friend, a human life like ours, truly and thoroughly human, sympathizing with ours yet more than ours, and above it, which seemed to be moving on a higher plane than ours, with a stronger faith than ours, better, purer, with a higher motive in it, guiding it, controlling it, transfiguring it, and seeming to us to come from a higher world than ours? Have we never had, every one of us, the vision of such a life, in some man, perhaps some woman, some person at least, who, as we stood before him, in his immediate presence, feeling then his power, his quickening influence resting then upon us, seemed to scatter and banish and drive away all our doubts and questions? Standing there before him we did not have any doubts. If we did for a moment, it was only to be ashamed of them. We did not think them then. We did not speak them then, for we were seeing then the vision of another life, of another world, of an open heaven, through the medium of a man! What that man himself believed, we did not know; we did not think to ask. Whether he was heterodox or orthodox we did not know; we did not care to know. We only knew that he seemed to us to be standing at the right hand of God.

Surely we have all had, sometime, somewhere, in the past, such a vision as that. Such a vision as that, my friends, is passing before the face of the civilized world to-day. The Christmas vision; on which the civilized world is beginning to-day to look, and which, as it looks upon it, scatters for a while at least, its shadows and its clouds; or which, by its brightness, resting on the clouds, piercing and pencilling the clouds, is making beautiful the clouds; and awakening somehow in the heart of the civilized world to-day, a peace, a joy, a gladness, like a stirring music thrill, too deep, too high, too big, too something great for words!

What is it the vision of? Of a man? Yes. Of a great, and good man? Yes; great and good, but greater than the greatest, higher than the highest, better than the best; coming to us strangely—it would be strange if He did not so come—in and through Whose vision another vision shines, as through the vision on the earth of no one else it shines; of another life, of another world, revealing to us God, His power, His authority, His sovereignty, His right hand reaching down and touching and resting on the earth; guiding, controlling the earth; helping us here to live, as here we ought to live, as here we want to live, with patience, with endurance, with courage, by opening heaven to us!

That is the Christmas vision. In larger and fuller measure that was the vision which Saint Stephen saw; the vision of heaven and God, but the vision of heaven and God through the medium of a man. As it came to him, so must it come to us, so must it come to all; not by the argument of a man, not by the philosophy of a man, not by the teaching or the preaching of a man, but by the *vision* of a man. And above all, by the vision of Jesus Christ, in Whom as in no one else we see the vision of God.

My friends, do we have that vision, of heaven and God, through Jesus Christ? If we do, then do we have and see the best, the brightest, the truest thing it is possible for us to see. And in the light of that vision, another vision we see; the vision of man in the future years, dwelling upon the earth, exalted, inspired, more and more redeemed, living in two worlds, this world and another, lifted up, standing as in an open heaven, at the right hand of God!

THE TWILIGHT VISION.

At evening time it shall be light.—ZECHARIAH xiv. 7.

THE TWILIGHT VISION.

The prophet in this chapter is describing what he calls the "day of the Lord." And a very strange day it is; opening, not in brightness like other days, and continuing in brightness to its close, but opening in darkness, or partial darkness at least, with some admixture of brightness in it, but not enough to dispel the darkness altogether. And yet—and this is the other strange thing about it—from this darkness, or from this partial darkness, brightness at last issues; so that, as the prophet tells us, "At evening time"—and it has all seemed like a kind of evening time—"At evening time it shall be light!"

Let us consider this characteristic of the day of the Lord, and see how it is that brightness comes from darkness, or what we learn in the twilight.

We sometimes hear it said, as an objection to the Christian religion, that if it be as it claims to be, a revelation to us, why does it not *reveal* what we would so much like to know? Why does it not reveal, more openly and clearly, so that there would be no mistake and no uncertainty about it, and no possibility of uncertainty or of mistake—why does it not reveal what we would all like to know, in such a way and fashion that we could not help knowing it? We would all like to know, for instance, a little more than we do, a great deal more than we do, about God Himself; Who He is, and what He is, and where He is. And some of us perhaps would like to know a great deal more than we do, beyond all doubt and question, whether He is at all. We would also like to know a great deal more than we do about the immortality of the soul, and another life, and another world. And if there be another world, what are the conditions of existence in that other world? How do people live there? What do people do when they get there? What shall we do when we get there, if we do get there? What shall we see there? Whom shall we meet and know there? Shall we meet and know our friends there, and recognize them there, and love and enjoy them there, and be with them there, in fellowship, forever? We think so; we hope so; we believe it. But we would like to believe it more. We would like to have it revealed to us in such a way that we could not help believing it; that nobody in all the world could help believing it. Would it not be better if it could be so revealed, if it had been so revealed; and would not we be better, more patient in our trials, more faithful in our duties: would not we be better?

Ah, would we? I do not believe we would, or could! I do not believe that in such a case there would be any such thing, or any such word as "better," in its moral sense. For "better" in its moral sense is a word that is associated with character; and I do not believe that in such a case there would be any such thing as character, or any such thing at least as the development of character. For how is character developed? Through knowledge? No; not exactly. Character is developed through the searching after knowledge, with peril, toil, risk, uncertainty, and the possibility of not finding it: through searching after knowledge is character developed. If the knowledge which we seek could be given to us without seeking it, it would be not a blessing but a calamity to us, a very great calamity, the greatest perhaps of any. But the world has been so wisely ordered and fashioned, this world in which we live, that whatever calamity we may experience in it, we cannot experience that calamity of finding knowledge without searching for it.

There is brightness in the world; there is darkness in the world; brightness mixed with darkness, a kind of twilight darkness, or a kind of twilight brightness; the brightness not so bright that we can see what we want to see if we do not make an effort to see; and the darkness not so dark that we cannot see what we want to see if we do make an effort to see. And out of this twilight brightness, or out of this twilight darkness, slowly, gradually, surely, character comes and issues, grows, strengthens, ripens, bears fruit, blesses and enriches both its possessor and the world.

That is man's distinctive place and function in the world; as midway in the world he stands, between the beasts and God;

> "Lower than God who knows all, and can all,
> Higher than beasts which know and can so far,
> As each beast's limit, perfect to an end,
> Nor conscious that they know, nor craving more,
> While man knows partly, but conceives beside,
> Creeps ever on, from fancies to the fact.
> And in this striving, this converting air,
> Into a solid he may grasp and use,
> Finds progress, man's distinctive mark alone,
> Not God's, and not the beasts: God is, they are,
> Man partly is, and wholly hopes to be."

And so, pressing on through the partial darkness around him—not too dark—or the partial brightness around him—not too bright—character comes and grows; shadowy at first, and vague in its outline, then real, solid, substantial, immortal—character, out of the twilight!

So does character always come to people. So did your character come. Such character as you now possess, whatever it may be worth, how did you come to possess it? Go back and try to recall, some of you men, your early days; some of you successful men who have prospered in the world. You were starting then on your journey. In order to make the illustration a little more concretely appealing, let us suppose—and it may not be altogether a fanciful supposition in the case of some of you—let us suppose it was a geographical journey. You had to cross the continent—quite a formidable thing in those days—and go to California; or you had to cross the ocean, also a formidable thing in those early days—and go to China or Japan. Did you see before you started the whole course of your journey, and all that it involved? You did not; you could not. Fortunately for you, you could not. Or, you saw it in the twilight, with brightness enough to see the possible safety in it, with darkness enough not to see the possible peril in it. And because of the brightness, and in spite of the darkness, you started on your journey, out into the twilight! As the result, you reached not only the place you wanted to reach—but, something else you reached! Facing and braving the peril, meeting and running the risk, going forth to wrestle with and to master and overcome the difficulty and the danger, something else you reached; skill, cleverness, intelligence, endurance, self-reliance, good judgment, *character* you reached, than which you nothing better and nothing richer reached.

So, throughout your whole journey, across the formidable continent, or the formidable ocean of life, if character be the goal we are meant to find and reach, there is no better way in which to reach and find it than just this twilight brightness, or just this twilight darkness, in which at present we are. The brightness not perfectly bright, but bright enough to encourage effort; the darkness not perfectly dark, but dark enough to require effort; and through the effort encouraged, or the effort required, character is reached, than which we can nothing better, and nothing richer reach.

Now, that is what the prophet calls the "day of the Lord"; a twilight day, an evening day, a day both bright and dark; that is what the prophet calls the "day of the Lord" on earth, the day in which the Lord of human hearts and lives makes Himself supreme in human hearts and lives, makes them more and more what they are meant to be. Out of the darkness brightness comes: at the evening time—it has all seemed like a kind of evening time—at the evening time, the light!

If that be true, that character is the goal of human life on earth, and that character grows, and expands, and is developed best in the twilight, then one or two things we learn that may help us a little.

We learn in the first place not to be surprised when we find that that is just exactly what the Christian religion is, or just exactly what the Bible is. A revelation? Yes: but a twilight revelation; not telling us all at once, or showing us all at once, with a quick and full illuminating flash, what we would all like to know. It would not be good for us, for our character, for our character development, if we did know it in such fashion. There is brightness in the Bible, divine brightness in it; there is brightness enough to show us what we ought to do, and what we ought to be; brightness enough to guide us and to help us in our present path. Well, then, let it guide us and more brightness will come. Shall I give an instance? Here is one: "Forgive your enemies." Do you all hear that? "Forgive your enemies." Is not that a divine thing, is not that a divine light in the Bible?

That is all the light, it seems to say, that some of you need just now. Never mind about those other things, God, and the soul, and the future life, and another world—you are not ready yet to know about those other things, to receive that other light. Here is this thing right before you, this light, "Forgive your enemies!" Let it shine upon you, in you, through you, making you light; and some more light will come! And out of what is now so dark visions will come and dawn, visions, of God, of the soul, of another life, of another world; and more and more will this Twilight Book be a book of visions to you.

One other thing: If character be the goal of human life on earth and character grows, and expands, and is developed best in the twilight, then we should not be surprised if sometimes in the brightness that has been upon our path, the darkness gathers around us, and the twilight gloom appears. Has it been so with some of you? I know it has. And do you sometimes ask and cry, with bitterness of heart, why it is so? Ah, my friends, there are some things that you never would have learned, never could have learned in the open sunshine; some things so great, so valuable, so true, that the God of human hearts and lives would have you learn and know them. The world has had its day with you, now the Lord is having His day with you, revealing His glory in you, drawing nearer to you, drawing you nearer to Himself. Out of the darkness brightness will come, and, at evening time, the light!

The evening time—yes, it is all a kind of evening time. But there is another evening time, which comes at the end of human life on earth, when the years behind us are many, and the years before us are few, and age comes on. Will it all be darkness, and feebleness, and frailness then? Or seeing then, perhaps, in a better perspective than now, what things are right, and good, shall not age have its vision as well as youth and manhood? Peace, patience, wisdom, faith, hope, love, and at evening time, the light!

THE VISION OF MYSTERY.

A priest forever, after the order of Melchisedec.—
HEBREWS viii. 17.

THE VISION OF MYSTERY.

The person here called Melchisedec is a mysterious character who suddenly appears to Abraham on his way to the promised land, gives his blessing to him, and then just as suddenly and abruptly disappears. Whence he comes, or whither he goes, we do not know. All we know is this: He comes, and blesses, and goes.

I want to show you this morning, if I can, that all the ministering forces of life come and go in the same manner, from mystery unto mystery, like priests after the order of Melchisedec; and that all we know about them is this: That they give their blessing to us, or may indeed be made to give their blessing to us.

First, and as preliminary to what I wish to say subsequently, let me speak of the ministering forces of nature. We are apt to think, or some of us are, in these days of the prevalence of the scientific spirit, that the mystery of the universe is gradually being resolved, dissipated, cleared up; and that the only thing that still stands for mystery, dealing as it were in mystery, trading in it, doing business with it, making capital out of it, is religion. A moment's reflection, however, will show us that that is not the case; and that the scientific spirit which is at present so dominant, instead of banishing mystery is revealing mystery—if that be not a paradoxical phrase—is revealing mystery to us, making us conscious more and more of the impenetrable mystery about us.

Take, for instance, that subtle and powerful force, which the scientific spirit is studying so much to-day, and making in so many ways such a useful force; not only as a mechanical force, changing our machinery; not only as an optical force, illuminating our buildings, and cities, but as a pathological force, revealing to us our bones! What blessings it has given, and will continue to give, innumerable, incalculable. Yes; but what is it? We call it "Electricity." But nomenclature is not knowledge. What is "Electricity"? Where, in its first analysis, does it come from? Whither, in its last analysis, does it go? We do not know. We cannot tell. All we can say is this: That it comes, blesses, and goes; from mystery unto mystery, like a priest after the order of Melchisedec. And that is all we know about it!

So with the other ministering forces of nature,

such as light, and heat, and gravity. What we know is this: That they appear, give a blessing to us, render a service to us, then disappear; like the bird that flew out of the dark into the lighted hall, and sang for a moment its blithesome song to cheer the hearts of the guests, and then flew out of the hall into the dark again.

So do they come, those ministering forces of nature; so also do they go; from mystery unto mystery; giving as they come, and go, their benediction to us, like priests after the order of Melchisedec. And that is all we know about them.

Or, if I were speaking in more strictly philosophical or scientific language, I would put it in this way: We only know phenomena, appearances, manifestations. The noumena, or the essences back of phenomena, we do not know, and never shall know, in this world.

Now, my friends,—and this is the point at which I have been aiming—if it be true of the ministering forces of nature, that all we know about them is not their first "whence," and not their last "whither," or what in themselves they are; but simply *that* they are; then, why should it be a surprise or an offence when we find that that is all we know about the ministering forces of religion? And yet to many it seems to be both a surprise and an offence. Religion, they say, is such a mysterious thing; there is so much in it that they cannot understand, so nebulous, and vague: it is such a mysterious thing! So it is. It comes from mystery, out of the bosom of impenetrable mystery, for it comes from a Being Whom we call "God," or professes to come from a Being Whom we call "God." And God,—who shall explain Him? Not only does it come from God, it also goes to God, carries us to God in thought, brings us to God in communion, binds us to God in conscience, with a sense of responsibility, calling upon us to love God, and to serve God, and to believe in God. From God, I say, they come, those ministering forces of religion. To God they also go; from mystery to mystery, like priests after the order of Melchisedec; giving as they come, and go, their benediction to us; and that is all we know about them!

But what of that? That is all we know about the ministering forces of nature, light, heat, gravity, electricity; that they give their blessing to us. But that is enough. And we take that blessing, and use it, which light, and heat, and gravity, and electricity give. We take that blessing, and are blessed by it a little, and are helped by it a little to reach some promised land. That is the wise thing to do, and the right thing to do. It would be wrong and foolish not to do it. And it is the wise thing and the right thing to do in regard to the ministering forces of religion; not to repudiate them and reject them, and to have nothing to do with them, because we cannot understand them; but to take the blessing which they give, and use it, to be cheered and comforted by it, to be heartened and strengthened by it, and to be helped upon our journey toward some promised land.

Now, I have made this parallel between what I call the ministering forces of nature and the ministering forces of religion, because it seems to be the impression of some that while they walk in the path of nature they walk in the light, and go openly; and that when they walk in the path of religion they walk in the dark, and go blindly. Is it so? Clearly, it seems to me, it is not so. Up to a certain point, and the same certain point, both paths are light. We see the blessings which the forces of nature give us; we see the blessings which the forces of religion give us. Up to that point both of them are light. Beyond that point both of them are dark, and the one as dark as the other; an impenetrable mystery enshrouds them.

There is still another point in the parallel. The forces of religion sometimes seem to go astray, and instead of blessing human life they have the effect sometimes to injure human life, with superstitions, and persecutions, and alienations, and separations, and bigotries, and intolerances, and cruelties. But what of that, again? The forces of nature sometimes have the effect not to bless but to injure human life; and the electricity in the black thundercloud, instead of being our servant, to help us, and to bless us, becomes at times our master, our cruel master, and kills us! And the heat that warms our bodies consumes at times our bodies! And the force of gravity breaks and destroys at times our bodies! And all the forces of nature become to us at times destructive forces of nature. And yet, because of the fact that they sometimes hurt and injure, we do not cease to use those ministering forces of nature; neither, though they sometimes hurt and injure, should we cease to use the ministering forces of religion. Our wisdom is still to use them, in the one case, as in the other; and to make them—as they come and go give their blessing to us.

That, my friends, is the wisdom which I preach to you this morning; not the wisdom which undertakes to clear up and dissipate and explain all the mysteriousness in religion; not the wisdom which undertakes to answer all the questions about religion which you can ask. I cannot do that. No one can do it. But the wisdom which would prove the reality of religion by the experience of the blessedness of it.

That, I say, is the wisdom which I preach to you this morning; and to two classes of persons among you I preach it.

First, to those of you who have come out into some open avowal and acknowledgment of religion. The way to prove to the world the reality of that religion is not chiefly by strife, and debate, and theoretical discussion, meeting thus as best you can the various objections to it. No; not in that way. But to show in yourselves the blessedness of religion. Go, and show what it can do; how it makes you strong in duty, high in character, true in conduct, modest in your womanhood, upright in your manhood; serving your fellow man, loving your fellow man, your neighbor as yourself, or trying at least to do so. And the world will see and say, "There is something in religion, in spite of its mysteriousness, there is something in religion and it will come at last to believe in the reality of religion.

To another class of persons listening to me now,

that is the wisdom I preach. I mean the class of persons who have not come into an open avowal and acknowledgment of religion, because they are doubtful about it, are asking questions about it, are always asking questions about it, and evermore coming out, by the same door that in they went. To you I also say, Go, practice religion. The questions which you cannot answer, and which no one can answer for you, let them alone for a time. Go, practice religion; do it; be it; live it; put it on and become it; and your doubts and questions will go. Out of religious experience religious vision will come, religious assurance will come, and religious faith will come!

And what is it to "practice religion"? Jesus Christ is religion. All the ministering forces of religion are gathered and centred in Him. Jesus Christ is religion; Whose great, wonderful, quickening personality has flashed across the plane of our human life, with strange beginning, with strange ending, from mystery unto mystery, like a priest after the order of Melchisedec; giving His blessing to us!

THE VISION OF DOUBT.

Lord, I believe: help Thou mine unbelief.—ST. MARK ix. 24.

THE VISION OF DOUBT.

THAT was the exclamation of the man in the Gospel story, whose child was afflicted with what was then regarded as a demoniacal possession, and who had brought him to Jesus Christ to be cured. He believed that Jesus Christ, by the exercise of His healing power, could cure his child. But he believed it, apparently, when he thought of it at a distance, in his distant home perhaps, before he came near to it; and then when he did come near to it, and thought of it as something about to be performed, actually performed, in making his afflicted child strong and well again, his faith trembled and weakened, for it seemed too good to be true, and he doubted what he believed.

That was his case. His case was not singular, but plural, very plural, including ours perhaps. Let us inquire and see, calling the subject this: Doubt Sometimes as a Sign of Coming near to Christ. Let me show you how.

You people to whom I speak this morning call yourselves Christians. So I presume you are, all of you. You are not all members of the Christian

Church—I wish you were, it would do you good. Nevertheless, in some real and true sense, and after some real and true fashion, you are a Christian people. You are not a Mohammedan people, or a Buddhist people, or a Pagan people; you are a *Christian* people. If somebody should tell you—speaking not in jest but in earnest, meaning what he said—that you are not a Christian people, that you are a Pagan or a Buddhist or a Mohammedan people, you would think it an affront and be disposed to resent it. You are *not* a Pagan people, you are *not* a Mohammedan people, you are *not* a Buddhist people; you are a *Christian* people. You do not believe in Paganism, you do not believe in Buddhism, you do not believe in Mohammedanism; you believe in Christianity.

Yes, so you do, at a distance, as the man in the Gospel story believed in the healing power of Christ, at a distance. How is it when you come near to it, to take it, to adopt it, to make it *your* Christianity, personally and practically yours, not simply as a good thing in general for others, but as a good thing in particular for you? "Blessed are the meek" as a good thing for you. "Blessed are the merciful: Blessed are the pure in heart: Blessed

talebearers and the strife-makers, but the *peace-
makers*—as a good thing for you. "Love your
neighbor as yourself: Forgive your enemies: Seek
first the kingdom of God," when you go down town
in the morning, when you come back again in the
evening. And all those other ideal things which
Christianity teaches, which Christianity is—how
does it seem to you then, when you come near to it,
to be guided by it, to be ruled by it, to be cured by
it, with all your worldly practicings and exercisings
to be exercised and cast out of you?

Do you still continue to believe in it just as
much as you did, or do you then begin to have
some little doubt about it, some little misgiving
about it, saying to yourself at times, "while it is all
very beautiful, and admirable, and very good and
true, when looked at from a distance, yet personally and practically and near to, it won't work, it
won't go, it won't do; it is *too* good."

I said that not all of you are members of the
Christian Church. Is not that the reason of it, or
one of the reasons at least, and the principal one
perhaps, especially in the case of some of you men?
You have great respect for Christianity; you show
it; you think it a good thing; you believe in it.
Most persons do, in some kind of Christianity—

most persons in Christendom, I mean. But you do not want to come into too close quarters with it. You do not want to make it *your* Christianity. Situated as you are situated, living as you are living, as you think you will have to go on living in this world, you doubt whether you can make it your Christianity. And, inasmuch as that is what you would have to do in becoming members of the Christian Church, you do not become members of the Christian Church. If you ever should take that step, you say, you would be very different from some members of the Church that you know. Indeed you would, perhaps from most of them. But then you do not take it, and the rest of us do not have the benefit of your illuminating example, your high, ideal, Christian life, showing us so consistently and so admirably what the Christian religion is. You do not take it; and why? Because—isn't this the real "because"?—when it comes to the actual living of that high, ideal Christian life, your faith in the practicability of it is weakened in you, a little; it is too high, too ideal, too good to be true—for you. At a distance, and theoretically, you believe in it. Practically, and near to, you are not quite so sure about it. And so you do not come near. Think it over, and see if that is not the reason!—Doubt sometimes a sign of coming near to Jesus Christ.

Let me give you another illustration. Sometimes the Christian religion comes near to us; not by any effort upon our part to make it come near, but without any effort upon our part to make it come near. Yet it comes near. As long as we can believe in the Christian God at a distance, we do not have much trouble in believing in Him; and the revelation of Him which Jesus Christ has given, as a good, loving Father God, caring for His children, we accept as true. That is the Christian faith; that is our faith. We see some things at times which are hard to reconcile with that Christian faith in a good loving Father God, painful things, distressing things, apparently cruel things, accidents, calamities, bereavements, many kinds of suffering, very sharp, very severe, very hard to bear, happening in the world. But as long as they happen far away, in Siberia or China or Africa, and do not come home to us, we are able still to regard them, not with indifference altogether, yet with acquiescence, as part of the Christian scheme, part of the Christian plan, symbolized by the cross, which, in His better wisdom, for the bettering of the world, the Christian God has devised. In spite of all those suffering things, we still continue to hold our faith, in the good Christian God. Sometimes they do come near, they strike home, they happen to us; and the things we see and read about we are made to feel, and the Christian plan or scheme, symbolized by the cross, reaches out and touches and takes and gathers us into its great comprehensive coils, its thick nebulous folds. We are no longer standing at a distance from it; we are near it, in it, part of it. The Christianity of the cross has come to us, to be our Christianity; and the cross which symbolizes it is our cross, and symbolizes us, our scourging, our wounding, our loneliness, our darkness, our seeming God-forsakenness, taking away our happiness, our peace, our comfort, our home, as though He did not care! Where then is our Christian faith? What has become of it? Do we hold it then, or do we let it go a little? I think we let it go a little; doubting for a time at least what we have believed. And why? Because we have come near to the Christian religion; we have penetrated to its inmost sanctuary, where the cross is! And the goodness which there is seen is too high for us, too ideal, too good. We can not understand it. Blinded by our tears it does not look like goodness, and we can only cry aloud, and say, "O, help our unbelief!" Doubt, sometimes as a sign that we are coming near to Christ!

Another illustration of a more general character let me give.

Why is it that so many of us to-day seem to be troubled so much with doubts of a historical or of a speculative character, concerning Jesus Christ, the message of Jesus Christ, the story of Jesus Christ, His birth and life and death, and what He taught and did, and how He came and went, as in the Gospel records we find that story told? Are not those records as worthy of credence now as they ever were? They are *more* worthy of credence now than they ever were. Every new discovery made, of parchment or of tablet, has tended to confirm them. True enough, as everybody knows, they are not the original records of the story of Jesus Christ. There are no original records of the story of Jesus Christ. They are not in existence. We do not have them. But neither do we have the original records of the annals of Julius Cæsar, or of the histories of Tacitus, or of the letters of Pliny, or of the Lives of Plutarch. They are not in existence; not one of them. Those we have are copies, some of them quite old, but none of them any older than the records which we have of the story of Jesus Christ, and many not so old. And the records which we have of the story of Jesus Christ are ten to one more numerous than the records which we have of any other writing or of any other writer in that ancient world. And the whole tendency, of modern criticism, for the past hundred years, has been, as in every scholarly critic seen, of every school of thought, in every civilized country, a tendency going to show that the records which we have of the story of Jesus Christ are faithful and true reproductions of the original records; and that those original records were written at the time to which they are assigned, and by the men to whom they are attributed; and who have given us the story of a life which they could not possibly have invented without supposing them to have been the most consummate literary artists that have ever appeared in the history of the world. And if they were not that, as surely they were not, then must we regard their story as genuine and true.

Why then do some of us doubt that story; the story of that life. that death, that wonderful life and death, and still more wonderful life again after death? Why do we doubt it? Because the proofs of it are so meagre? No, because they are *not* so meagre. Because they are so few? No, because they are *not* so few. Because, by means of all these evidential processes, so voluminous, so varied, so indisputable, these critical inquiries, these historical investigations, these manuscript discoveries, these documentary findings; because, by means of all these new and opening paths, we are travelling back across the centuries, and coming very near to Jesus Christ to-day.

Never was any age, since His own contemporary age, so near to Jesus Christ as is this present age. Never did any age, since His own contemporary age, know so much of Jesus Christ as does this present age. And standing to-day as in His presence, we find it hard to believe in Jesus Christ, as the people in His presence did when He was on the earth. And we, like them, are dazzled by the brightness of His vision, so very bright, so ideally bright, so transcendentally and divinely bright, that it darkens and obscures! So good it seems, with its great, quickening hopes, its illuminating visions, its sublime declarations that we find it hard to credit it; too good it seems to be true!

That is the significance of much of the doubt which by this age is felt. It is a sign that the age is coming near to Jesus Christ, and receiving a vision of Him. Nearer still will it come, rising above its doubts, or pushing through its doubts, leaving its doubts behind, and finding at last, that what for a time it doubted because it seemed so good, too good indeed to be true, is just as true as good.

So did the man in the Gospel story find it. So have some of us found it. So more and more will many others find it. If on any of you, the darkness now is resting, of some bewildering experience which you cannot understand, or some bewildering problem which you cannot solve, do not become careless or hopeless; do not become hard and callous and worldly. Stand by your highest ideals! Hold them fast; do not let them go! Let them still persist in you. And from that darkening doubt a morning light will dawn, a deeper peace will issue, a stronger faith will come! You too shall find that the ideal is the real, is always the real, and that what is best is true. And Jesus Christ is real, and Jesus Christ is true; not a beautiful dream, dreamed by the world in its childhood long ago, and floating down through the ages, but which now, in its awakening manhood, the world is pushing aside—No, not a dream. Yet it is a dream: it is the dream on earth of God, in a real life, with bodily parts and members, having hands and feet, which more and more will guide and inspire and illumine the world, and lift it up more and more to righteousness and God, casting out and exorcising more and more all the evil things and evil spirits in it!

VISION BOOKS.

The book of the vision of Nahum the Elkoshite.—
NAHUM i. 1.

VISION BOOKS.

THIS you recognize as the prefatory and descriptive title of one of the books of the Bible. It may with equal propriety be regarded as the prefatory and descriptive title of every other book of the Bible, both of the Old Testament and the New— the book of the vision of David, the book of the vision of Isaiah, of Jeremiah, of Malachi, of Saint Paul, and Saint Peter and Saint John. Each of these persons wrote in a book what in passing through the world he was able to see in the world, then gave that book to the world, or left it behind him in the world, as his vision book, to the world.

That, it seems to me, is what each of us is doing, as I will try this morning to show you; giving, each of us, to the world, some vision book of the world.

One of the first questions that people are apt to ask us when we have visited and travelled through some strange and interesting country, is "What did you see there? What impressed you the most while there, engaged the most your attention, excited the most your interest; what impressed you most? What did you see?"

It is a natural question to ask; it is a natural question to answer. And in various ways and fashions we try to answer the question; sometimes by writing letters when we are on the journey; sometimes, if we are endowed with literary instinct and ability, by writing books after we have returned from the journey, which may be regarded as our " vision books " of the journey, or our vision books of the country through which we have made the journey.

Now, there is one strange and interesting country, very strange and very interesting, through which we are all passing even when we stay at home and do not travel at all; and that is the world itself. We have never been here before, at least I presume we have not, or not at all events in the same shape and fashion in which we are here now; we shall never be here again. This is our only journey in and through the world. And the question that people ask, is " What do you see on the journey?" They do not always ask it in just those words, perhaps; nevertheless they ask it, for they, too, are making the journey, and they want to get all the help and light about it they can; and therefore they ask of us, and we ask of one another, "What do you see on the journey? What are you able to see?" And in one way or another, whether or not we realize it, we are all answering that question, we are writing books about it, not with pen and ink and mechanical type, yet nevertheless we are writing books about it. Our lives themselves are the books, our aims, our efforts, our ambitions in the world; the things we try to do, and think it best to do, and most worth while to do; our lives themselves are the books, our vision books of the journey, or our vision books of the world through which we are making the journey; not the vision books of the apostles and prophets, of Jeremiah and Malachi and Saint John and Saint Paul, not *their* vision books of the world, but *our* vision books of the world. Or, if you please, they are our bibles, which people read and study, and get their inspiration from, sometimes their desperation! However much they may fail to read and study today those other and earlier Bibles by apostles and prophets written, they read and study our bibles, the bibles written by us, revealing to the world or to the people in the world how we view the world, and what upon the whole we see the world to be. They are our vision books of the world.

What kind of vision books are they, good ones or bad ones, right ones or wrong ones, true ones or false ones? What are the visions worth? We cannot surely say; but some day, so we are told, those vision books will be opened, more fully opened than now, their contents more fully disclosed and tested by some infallible judgment test as to their permanent value and worth. Then we shall see and know, not perhaps till then, what our visions are worth, and whether or not, or to what extent, we have been mistaken in them.

In order, however, that we may be as little mistaken as possible then, let us look for a few moments at some of our visions now, or some of our vision books.

There is first of all the physical vision book, or the physical vision by us of the physical world about us. And that is the vision of the world, and the only vision of it, or the principal vision of it, which some of us seem to have, the only kind of vision of it which we seem to show, and which, as in a book, our lives to-day reveal. It may be a little book, a poor, cheap, little book, not worth much, with but few pages in it, and not much written on them, constituting the record of a poor career in the world, which does not look as we read it like any career at all. Or it may be a large and sumptuous book, elegantly bound, with many pages in it, illuminated and rich, with many great achievements and many great successes written upon those pages; a large and sumptuous book. And yet, whether little or large, it is simply a book that reveals the physical world about us, with the physical pleasures in it, and the physical treasures in it, physical titles and tenures and properties and fortunes. That is the kind of vision, that is the kind of world, which as in a book the lives of some of us reveal. When that book is opened at last, what will its vision be worth? Valuable now as it seems to be, will it have any value then?

But some there are who give us another kind of vision, of another kind of world; which, as in a book, their lives also reveal. It is the poet's vision book, the artist's vision book, the student's, the scholar's, the thinker's vision book, to whom the physical forms of the physical world about them are simply forms of thought, in which that thought is bodied forth and clothed and expressed. These are the men and women who lift us up to see some ideal world, and make us feel the reality beyond this physical world, of some ideal world; who, in connection with the physical world about us, give us

> "The sense sublime
> Of something far more deeply interfused,
> Whose dwelling is the light of setting suns,
> And the round ocean, and the living air,
> And the blue sky; and in the mind of man
> A spirit and a motion that impels
> All thinking things, all objects of all thought."

These are the men and the women who somehow make us feel that the music which on earth with the physical ear we hear, is but the physical voicing of a music which with the physical ear we are not able to hear. That the beauty which with the physical eye we see, is but the physical flash of a beauty which with the physical eye we are not able to see. That all the light that breaks with pulsing morning flush or evening twilight glow over land or sea, is but the physical radiance or adumbration thereof a light that never was as yet on either land or sea!

These are the gifted men and women among us; poets, artists, students, scholars, thinkers, dreamers we sometimes call them, who lift us up I say to some ideal world, and make us feel the reality of that ideal world, which as in a book their lives to-day reveal. And when that book is opened at last, what will that vision be worth? Insubstantial as now it seems, will it be substantial then?

There is still another and higher vision which

some people have to-day, which does not seem connected much with any kind or form of physical sense within them. There is living at present in New York City a young girl, who is deaf and dumb and blind. Can you imagine it? Take it in slowly,— deaf, and dumb, and blind; with only the sense of touch! But wonderful things does she see! I doubt if there is any one else in all New York City who sees such wonderful things, such beautiful things, so wonderfully and beautifully true, and felt at once to be true when she reveals them to us, as Helen Keller sees![1] It is the vision of a soul, shining through the face, lighting up the face, and bodied forth with a voice she has been taught to speak, but which she cannot hear. The vision of a soul, seeing and apprehending, with its fine spiritual sense, that kingdom of God in the world, which you and I, my friends, with all our physical senses, and because of them perhaps, trusting in them so much, relying upon them so much, cannot so clearly see, and sometimes doubt and question and do not see at all!

It is the vision of a soul, apprehending more or less, and bearing witness to, that spiritual world about us for which religion stands, and which, by

[1] She was living in New York when this sermon was preached.

faith and prayer and worship and praise and song, and every sort of religious rite, purifying the soul and clarifying the soul, men and women have tried in all the ages to see, which you and I try to see, and sometimes do, a little. And moments of vision there are, in our highest moods and best, when the slumbering soul within us seems to feel the power of some awakening touch; and when breaking away from the prison bars of sense and outward things, it seems to be moving about for a time "in worlds not realized" by the physical faculties in us.

We have all had such moments. And yet, as we know too well, they are only fleeting moments, and that the vision does not stay. Once, however, there was seen a soul upon this earth, clothed and bodied forth in flesh and blood like ours, but shining through that flesh and blood and transfiguring with its radiance the bodily form that encased it, and revealing to men the beauties, the wonders, the realities of a kingdom of God about them, and whose life like no other that has ever lived was the vision book of God. It was the vision of Jesus Christ; in the light of which, as we walk in it, we too shall see and feel and shall ourselves reveal to the world, within, around and above the world, a more enduring world.

These are the vision books; the vision book of the eye, the vision book of the mind, the vision book of the soul, the vision book of Jesus Christ. When these books are opened at last, which of them will be found the truest and the best: that is the question which you and I, now, each for himself, must somehow try to determine.

THE CHRISTIAN VISION IN US.

Christ in you, the hope of glory.—COLOSSIANS i. 27.

THE CHRISTIAN VISION IN US.

In the chapter from which these words are taken, Saint Paul has been describing at considerable length the greatness of Jesus Christ. He calls Him the image of the Invisible God, in Whom all the fullness of the Invisible God appears, the Firstborn from the dead, the Firstborn of all creation, by Whom all things were made, in Whom they all consist. That is strong language to use, even of one who has proved himself as great as Jesus Christ; and we read it now, as the world has always read it, with some degree of astonishment. But how much greater is the astonishment when we find it used, not only with reference to Jesus Christ, but with reference to others; and that after Saint Paul describes, so vividly and graphically, the wonderful manifestation of the power and wisdom of God in the historical Jesus Christ, he says to those to whom he writes, "This Jesus Christ is in you."

It is of that—not Jesus Christ in history, not Jesus Christ in the Bible, but Jesus Christ in *you*, that I wish to speak.

You remember when upon one occasion our Lord

was holding a colloquy with the Jews, He said, to their surprise, "Your father Abraham rejoiced to see my day; he saw it and was glad." And when they turned and said, "Thou art not yet fifty years old, and hast thou seen Abraham?" He said, to their still greater surprise, "Verily I say unto you, Before Abraham was, I am." That is usually taken to mean that Jesus Christ was Divine, that Jesus Christ was God, that He did not begin to exist when first He appeared in history, but that He has always existed, is self-existent, as God is; that there never was a time when He began to be; that there never will come a time when He will cease to be; and that like God, He can say of Himself, I am.

Well, it does mean that, I think. Yet something else it means. Let me illustrate. The little tree that grew, and bloomed and blossomed and ripened and brought its fruit to perfection upon that distant plain of Mamre, where the patriarch Abraham lived, was in one sense a distinct, separate and individual tree, existing by itself and apart. And yet, when we remember what our physical science has taught us and caused us now to know, so vividly to know, that everything in the vegetable world which ever did exist, is vitally connected with everything else in the vegetable world which exists now or ever shall exist. When we remember I say that all the vital forces that energized and worked in the vegetable world of the past are energizing and working in the vegetable world to-day; then, of that little tree upon the plains of Mamre long ago it might be truly said, *it* might say, imputing human speech and human vision to it, that in looking upon the power that was working and growing in it, it saw indeed the power that would thereafter work, that would thereafter grow, in something else than it, and bigger and more than it. It saw in itself the power, it saw in itself the principle, it saw in itself the life that works and grows and blooms in all the varied glory of our summer life to-day. It saw it in itself, that summer bloom and beauty; it saw it in itself; it saw it and was glad. As all this summer beauty and summer bloom might say, "Before that tree in Mamre was, before any tree was, when nothing existed in all the world but one little germ of a tree, then, now, always, in it all, *I am;* one growth, one beauty, one bloom, one principle of life; in it all, *I am.*"

Something like that is what I also understand Jesus Christ to have meant when He said to the

Jews, "Your Father Abraham rejoiced to see my day, and he saw it and was glad." Not merely that He existed before Abraham: that is true; but that He existed *in* Abraham, that the moral and spiritual beauty, that the moral and spiritual power which struggled out in Abraham toward expression long before, is the same moral and spiritual beauty, bloom, power, which in all its fullness in Jesus Christ is seen, which existed before Abraham and since Abraham; which, as the manifestation of God in all human life on earth, then, now, always, can say of itself, "*I am*."

That is what Saint John elsewhere declares, when, in speaking of Jesus Christ upon one occasion, he says, "That was the true light which lighteth every man that cometh into the world." Every man, in other words, has Jesus Christ within him, feebly to be sure, and poorly, with much to obscure and hinder the manifestation of Him. And yet it *is* Jesus Christ. Just as the little ray of light that struggles in through yonder crack in the door, or through these painted windows, upon our faces here, is the same light whose golden garment wraps the earth in all its beauty to-day, whose arrows pierce the air, whose colors paint the cloud, whose beauties adorn the midnight sky, and which in the sun itself so fully and brightly shines that if we look directly at it or upon it our eyes are dazzled by it. Even so is the light, the moral and spiritual light, which struggles through the little cracks and windows in every human heart and soul, and which is never extinguished there, the same moral and spiritual light which, in all its beauty and splendor, in Jesus Christ is seen. Hence it was that Saint Paul, like his comrade apostle Saint John, after giving such a picture, such a vivid and graphic picture of the glory of Jesus Christ, a glory so great, so bright, so overwhelmingly bright that it has dazzled the gaze of the world, which apart from all the creeds, has seemed to make men feel as they looked upon Him that they saw Him to be the image of the Invisible God; could write to the people then, and say, "This Jesus Christ is in you!"

So does Saint Paul teach, so does Saint John teach, so does the Bible teach, so does the Christian religion teach, "Jesus Christ is in you!" This then is the truth which in the text we find.

What does it signify? What is its practical value? It gives a new name and a new meaning to human life, or rather to that principle of righteousness which struggles in human life. It takes all the righteousness which in the world we find, no matter where we find it, in Greece or Rome or Egypt or Babylon or Palestine or Jerusalem or New York, no matter where we find it, then, there, here, and puts the name and stamp of Jesus Christ upon it. Wherever in all this world men are fighting hard against evil forces, struggling, wrestling with them, trying to overcome them, *there* is the wilderness where Jesus Christ is fighting. Wherever men are trying hard to be patient in trial, patient in sorrow, in suffering, in loss, trying to be submissive and to drink some bitter cup, *there* is the Gethsemane where Jesus Christ is patient, and saying, "Thy will be done." Wherever men are dying for principle and truth, sacrificing themselves for the good of their fellow men; or where, with clouds and darkness gathered round about them, unable to see, to understand, they are trusting still in God, *there* is the Calvary where Jesus Christ is crucified, and the cross on which He dies! Wherever in this world we see, no matter what men call it, nobleness and truth, purity of heart, moral and spiritual courage, honor, manhood, righteousness; it is all one honor, one manhood, one righteousness; Jesus Christ is what it means, and Jesus Christ is the name of it.

Thus does the truth contained in the text take the story of Jesus Christ and spread it over the world, making it the world's story, the world's great drama, with Jesus Christ appearing again on the stage of human life, our human life to-day, our struggling human life, struggling toward the truth, struggling toward the right, and giving thus to our struggling life its meaning and its name. Jesus Christ its meaning, Jesus Christ its name. It gives a new meaning to us.—It gives a new purpose to us, something to live for. Yes, men and women, something to live for. In all places, in all circumstances, in winter days and summer days, in frost and cold and heat, in the city and in the country, dwelling in the forest or dwelling by the sea; or whatsoever happens of sorrow or joy, of sunshine or cloud, of brightness or of darkness; something to live for, always to live for, always worth while to live for; a motive to inspire us and a goal at which to aim. And that is to develop and to bring out more and more, wheresoever placed, the Jesus Christ within us; and thus to feature more and more His image in ourselves. Then do we find, all of us and always something to pursue. Then do we find our trade, our calling, our business, our real and true business in life. That is where your business is, the business of you men. It is not down-town or perhaps up-town, where your stores and shops and offices and banks are, and where you are trying so hard to get on and to make money. That is not your real and true business. Nor is it my real and true business to preach and make sermons and to look after Saint Bartholomew's Parish and Saint Bartholomew's Parish House. We have another business than that, greater and more important. And whether we work in stores or factories or shops or offices or banks, whether we preach in pulpits, whether we sing in choirs, or simply manage our home affairs, our home concerns and duties and social undertakings and functions and engagements, it is all the same business, we are all in it together, we are all partners in it,—the business of bringing out more and more, wherever placed, the Jesus Christ within us, thus causing more and more Jesus Christ to appear, not as a fact in history which happened long ago, but as a fact in us, and which is happening now.

That is our chief business in life. That is our principal purpose in life. That is our power in life. That is our usefulness in life. That is the way in which we do the greatest good in life; not through our intellectual gifts, not through our physical gifts of endowment or possession, but through ourselves, or through the Jesus Christ developed within ourselves. A long and great and illustrious career came to a close the other day in Hawarden Castle in Wales; and the whole English Nation, the whole British Empire, the whole civilized world moved and stirred by a common impulse, is paying now, its mournful yet grateful tribute to him. And to whom is it paying the tribute? Not to the brilliant statesman who, for more than half a century, has been such a conspicuous figure and factor in National and International affairs. Not to the gifted orator whose voice could so easily charm, as it has so often charmed, and swayed and moved the people, with "th' applause of listening senates to command." Not to the acute dialectician, the versatile genius, the thinker, the student, the scholar, the great forensic debater, the great Parliamentary leader, but to Gladstone, the Man, the Christian man, whom, now that he is gone both friends and foes alike—for many foes he had, implacable and bitter—are uniting to honor. Who, in the course of a long and varied career, tried steadfastly more and more to feature in himself the image of Jesus Christ, making that from first to last his principal purpose in life, the secret of his power then, and of his influence forever: Gladstone, the man, the Christian Man!

Jesus Christ in you, giving to you your meaning, giving to you your purpose, giving to you your power, giving to you your hope. For what must be the end of such a life? Must it go out and perish? That is not the story. That is not the end of the story, or not at least the end of the story of the life of Jesus Christ. That life goes on and up; it rises and ascends, it must. How otherwise, simply as a literary picture, could any one portray it? It passes on into a greatness, a brightness, a glory, so great and bright that we cannot with our vision follow it, into something so great and bright that we are not able to picture or to dream it. But it rises, goes on, ascends,—that is the story. That is the end of it. Make that story yours, men and women; try to, honestly, sincerely try to, as far as now you can, follow it and trace it, finding in it your meaning, finding in it your purpose. Then will the end of that story be the end of your story. With a great and growing conviction will you know that your story will have no end. Passing out of sight, yet not passing away, rising, ascending, going on into something else and more, that the heart of man hath not conceived, nor the eye of man seen, but singing, sounding in you now, as the hope of glory in you.

What is the glory? Will it be the glory of a fully developed intellectual life, when we shall see and know as we are seen and known, apprehending truth, not in its fragmentariness but in its entireness? Will it be the glory of the moral life, where we can do what now we wish to do but are not able to do? Will it be the glory of the spiritual life, where all the thoughts and feelings by sweetest music stirred, shall come out into expression?

> "Life's helm rocks to the windward and lea,
> And Time is as wind, and as waves are we;
> And song is as foam that the sea winds free,
> Though the thought at its heart may be deep as the sea."

Where those deep thoughts and feelings touched and awakened by music shall come out, and we shall sing a new song? Will it be the glory of the fully developed social life, where the hindered fellowships and broken friendships shall all be gathered up and united? I do not know; you do not know; but something very bright and beautiful will it be; singing, sounding in you now, as the hope of glory in you.

THE VISION OF THE DIVINE PURPOSE.

The son of man goeth as it is written of him.—
ST. MATTHEW xxvi. 24.

THE VISION OF THE DIVINE PURPOSE.

Do these words of Jesus Christ imply a want of knowledge upon His part, of the divine destiny that awaits him? Possibly not; but they do seem to imply that such knowledge is neither necessary nor desirable. It is quite enough to know, so He seems to say, that there is in the book of God for Him, something written down, which He is interpreting and fulfilling, and that the Son of man goeth: How? Where? As it is written of him.

That was enough for Him. That is enough for us; and not only enough, but best. It is of that this morning that I wish to speak—The Fulfilling of God's Scripture Concerning Us. In order, however, that we may appreciate that, and the significance of it, let me first speak of something else.

What is it that gives to our human life its chief inspiration and value? Not any outward circumstance, or state or occasion or condition, though these things of course are important factors in it. But there is something more important, more vitally important. It is I think the consciousness upon the part of human life of *something to live for*, something worth while to live for, that is always worth while to live for, and for which we can go on with an ever-increasing zest of keenest delight, to live. Whatever takes away that consciousness from life, that sense of purpose from it, makes the life less vital. Whatever gives or imparts that consciousness to life, that sense of purpose to it, makes the life more vital.

Is there anything that is taking away that consciousness from our life to-day, that sense of purpose from it? Yes, I think there is. What is it? *Our prosperity is taking it away.* Does that seem like a strange statement to make? Perhaps it does. And yet, if we reflect upon it for a little while, we shall find I think that it is true—that the tendency of a prosperous life, considered by itself, with nothing else in it to counteract that tendency, is toward a purposeless life; its prosperity neutralizing its purpose, by consummating its purpose, or if not by consummating it, by dissipating it, militating against the singleness of its energy, and weakening more or less its propelling force by scattering its aim!

Take the case, for example, of some one prosperous man. It is not hard for some of you to take such a case. He was not always prosperous. There was a time when he was not prosperous. He had his way to make in the world, by toil, and effort, and purpose; by persistent effort and purpose, saying to himself resolutely, "This one thing I do, and must do, in order to get on." And now he has "got" on. And the things which once he tried so hard to reach and gain, he has in a measure gained. What is the result? Having gained in a measure the things, he has lost in a measure the purpose by which he gained the things. He does not feel it now as he felt it then. He does not have it now as he had it then. And with perhaps the same strong ambition in it—though that I think is doubtful—there is not the same sharp and severe necessity in it. That part of his purpose is gone. That part of his purpose was a very important part, a very essential part; its quickening force and nerve vitalizing it, vitalizing him; keeping it alive when otherwise it would have died; keeping him alive when otherwise he would have died, and enabling him thus to become at last the prosperous man that he is.

And having in that way, by that necessitous purpose, become a prosperous man, he is not now in that way, and that necessitous purpose is not in him now. His prosperousness has destroyed it, or at all events impaired it and made it feeble in him.

That is the tendency of prosperity—toward the enervating of purpose by the consummating of purpose. That is the penalty which we have to pay for it, which the prosperous man has to pay, which the prosperous society has to pay, which the prosperous age has to pay, which this age has to pay, which it is paying—the penalty of the impairment of purpose for the reward of the fulfillment of purpose. And so, the prosperity of this age, in taking from it its quickening and vitalizing purpose, may be its adversity!

Then look again, not at some of the older men to-day, who, because of prosperous *development*, are without much purpose in life, but at some of the younger men to-day, who, because of prosperous *inheritance*, are without much purpose in life. They do not have to toil for bread. Therefore they are apt to conclude, some of them—jumping over a suppressed premise—that they do not have to toil. And the suppressed premise is this: THAT WHENEVER A MAN IS SO SITUATED IN THIS WORLD THAT HE DOES NOT HAVE TO TOIL FOR BREAD, HE MUST ALL THE HARDER TOIL FOR SOMETHING ELSE THAN BREAD; and that only by the sweat of his brow, his brain, his intellect, can he escape the curse in life, and find the blessing in it! It is a law, like that which holds the stars in their course, which no man can break with impunity. Some of the younger men of this generation seem to be breaking it, but not with impunity. Instead of working, toiling all the more, with some high purpose, at some high task, for the good of the country, for the good of the world, because they are so circumstanced that they *can* toil all the more, with such high purpose, at such high task, they are not toiling much at any particular task, with any particular purpose, except at the task at which they do not need to toil!

It is not so with all; but it is so with a many, and the tendency of their prosperous life is toward a purposeless life.

Is it any better with young women to-day? They come out of school, where they had a purpose, which meant to them so much more than they were aware of at the time, not only in forming and developing their minds, but in vitalizing their lives. Now they come out of school; and then what? Yes, and then what? They do not have to toil, the young women of whom I speak. They do not have to be breadwinners, the young women of whom I speak. What is their purpose in life? We know of course what that consummation is which most of them reach and find and are intended to reach and find, but it is hardly a very dignified or a very seemly or a very womanly thing for them to be aiming with self-directed purpose and intent toward that consummation, figuring and finessing always toward that consummation. Yet what else is there to do? I am often asked the question, I am asked it every week, sometimes every day in the week, and sometimes a great many times in a day—How is a young woman to live to-day who has to earn her bread? It is not always an easy question to answer. But there is another question much harder to answer —How is a young woman to live to-day who does *not* have to earn her bread? What is her purpose? If she were poor she would have one; a hard one perhaps and difficult to perform, but she would have one. But she is not poor, and therefore she has none.

And so, my friends, we see, whether we look at the matter theoretically or whether we look at it practically, that the prosperousness of our modern life, inherited or acquired, is apt to take away, by consummating it or by dissipating it, and in either case by neutralizing it, the sense of purpose from it.

What is it then that can give this sense of purpose to us, to all of us to-day, and not only give it but keep it; the sense of something to live for, of something worth while to live for, that is always worth while to live for, for which we can go on, with ever-increasing zest of keenest joy, to live? Here it is: "The Son of man goeth as it is written of him." Here is the sense of purpose, for that Son of man, for every son of man. It is the sense of a purpose of God, sending him into the world, sending us into the world, sending everybody into the world; not for nothing—no, no, that cannot be. If there be an Infinite Wisdom in the universe, then are we sent into the world not for nothing but for something. What is that something? We do not know. You do not know. I do not know. There is not anybody who does know. It is not necessary for him to know. It is not desirable for him to know. It is desirable for him not to know. It is enough for him to know, and not only enough but best, that there is in the book of God for him something written down, which is to be by him, through him, in him interpreted and expressed, and which cannot be in him expressed except as he does not know what it is; except as, day after day, he watches, diligently, sensitively, sympathetically, watches for it to come. In that way he grows into it, or it grows into him, becomes embodied in him, revealed and expressed. Just as the scholar or the pupil is enabled thus to express, is enabled thus to embody, the purpose of his teacher. Not by knowing clearly and at the outset the whole content of the purpose of his teacher concerning him; he does not know that, and cannot, and it would not be good for him to know it; but simply by knowing the fact that the teacher has in his book for him, something written down, some thought, some knowledge, some purpose, some ideal purpose; and then by watching diligently, sympathetically, for that purpose to come, in the tasks which the teacher assigns day after day, and so going day after day as it is written of him.

Well, pupils of God we are, in His school, the school of that Infinite Wisdom which made and orders the universe, and enfolds us all in its great comprehensive embrace; which, because it is Infinite Wisdom, sends us into the world for something, with something written down in the book of God concerning us, which we should try to become, which we can become, not by knowing what it is, but simply by knowing *that* it is; and then looking for it, in all the daily tasks which we take up in the morning, and follow through the fleeting hours from breakfast-time to bedtime. That something for us of God, pure, worthy, good, ideally worthy and good; looking for it, sensitively, sympathetically, thus gradually finding it, revealing it, becoming it, and so going day after day—Where? How? To what? As it is written of us.

That, we must all admit, is theoretically, the purpose of human life. If it should become in fact the purpose of human life to-day, what would it do for human life? It would, without arresting its prosperous trend and course, arrest indeed and check its purposeless trend and course, giving and imparting to human life to-day the sense of something to live for, causing it to say or to feel, while doing many things, yet "This one thing I do"; while moving about in many paths, in many different ways, yet "This one way I go;—as it is written of me." Yes, something worth while to live for, always worth while to live for, would it give and impart with the feeling that something better and more is coming all the time, and then with a deep and growing wonder we would be always watching for that something to come. And so going through the days fulfilling the scripture of God concerning us, trying to bear our crosses and to stand up under our burdens, to be patient and brave in the midst of the irritating and annoying things, to be humble, unselfish, pure in heart, in the midst of the great, and prosperous things;—in all things, that the scripture of God concerning us might be fulfilled, and clinging always to that as the one great purpose in life. With many temptations to live a baser and lower life, and disposed at times to yield, we would be fortified with the thought; how then can the scripture of God concerning us be fulfilled?

So, like Jesus Christ, might every son of man go through his days with the consciousness of something to live for, gathering up all the fragments of his broken life, and bringing them together in one unfolding purpose, that is always worth while, and more and more worth while. Thus entering into life here, thus passing through it here, thus going from it here,—How? Where? To what? No matter! going as it is written of us, and that the scripture of God concerning us may be fulfilled.

THE VISION OF THE DIVINE METHOD;

OR

BONDAGE, FREEDOM AND OBEDIENCE.

God spake all these words, saying, I am the Lord thy God, which have brought thee out of the land of Egypt, out of the house of bondage.—EXODUS XX. 1, 2.

THE VISION OF THE DIVINE METHOD:

OR

BONDAGE, FREEDOM AND OBEDIENCE.

These words constitute, as you know, the introduction to the Ten Commandments, which God gave through Moses to the children of Israel at Sinai. They had been delivered from Egypt, where they were in bondage; they had been led out into the Wilderness, where they were free; they had been brought at last to Sinai, where the effort was made to teach them to obey. Egypt, the Wilderness, Sinai; Bondage, Freedom, Obedience. That was the Divine method of development in the case of the Jewish people. It is, or it seems to be, the Divine method of development in the case of every people, and it is of that Divine method of development that I purpose this morning to speak.

The movement which originated in the Sixteenth Century in Europe, or which if not originating then was made conspicuous then, which then came up to the surface, was a movement toward freedom, toward religious freedom, delivering men and women from the Ecclesiastical house of bondage. But it did not stop there. Having once started it went on. The people had tasted freedom; it tasted good. They wanted more freedom, from more houses of bondage, social, civic, economic, mental, moral, circumstantial; from more houses of bondage. The movement went on, deepening, widening, strengthening; has since been going on, is going on now. "Freedom" is now the cry, the rallying cry of the world, inspiring the world, inflaming the world, exhilarating the world, sometimes exhilarating it too much; making the world drunk, with freedom! Human life to-day, having been delivered from its old bondage houses, is out in the Wilderness going wild with freedom there, or going wild about it. The part of human life that is not yet there is trying hard to get there, and is getting there more and more, to freedom. Not for the sake of what freedom indeed can do, but just for the sake of freedom; sporting there, with freedom; playing there, with freedom; a dangerous thing to play with; yet playing there, revelling there, carousing there, with freedom, from the old coercive restraints, from the old coercive economies, customs, laws, conventions!

That is where our human life seems to be to-day;

not in Egypt, that belongs to the past from which it has been delivered; not at Sinai, the Mount of Obedience, that belongs to the future to which it has not yet come; but in the Wilderness, between them. Does it not seem so? Look and see. Look within, some of you, within yourselves and see. The old religious beliefs, the old religious theories, which once you found within yourselves, to hold you, to keep you, to bind you fast—do you find them now within you? Do you find them now so much? Do they hold you now so much? Do they bind you now so much? Or have you got away from them a little, perhaps a great deal? And if you have got away from them a little or a great deal, what have you put in their place? Have you put anything in their place? Or are you just out in the Wilderness, free indeed from what you once believed, and thought and had and held; *free*, and that is all; just free, with the freedom of the Wilderness, bewildering you at times, perhaps frightening you at times, causing you almost to feel at times as though you would like to go back into the old house of bondage again, with its old tasks and taskmasters, harsh and hard as they were, and yet so clearly prescriptive of things to think and believe and do. But you cannot go back. The Wilderness shuts you off and shuts you in. And that is where your inner life seems to-day to be; not in Egypt, that belongs to the past from which you have been delivered; not at Sinai, that belongs to the future to which you have not yet come; but in the Wilderness between them!

Does it not seem so? Look again; not at the life within, but at the life without. Look at the life of the State, the modern State, and see how freedom to-day is apotheosized, deified, made into a god, doing wonders, working miracles; where folly becomes wisdom, where bad becomes good, where wrong becomes right. How? Not by the slow, labored process of a growth, but by the quick, free process of a vote, a popular vote, unenlightened, perhaps unintelligent, but no matter; a popular vote has done it. As though there were in a vote, a free and popular vote, some thaumaturgic power, some miraculous power, some instantaneously transforming power, changing all at once darkness into light, blackness into white—Freedom becoming a god, more than a god, doing what God cannot do; making that right which had not been right before, making that good which had not been good before!

That is where the life of the State, the modern State, seems to-day to be; not in Egypt, from which it has been delivered; not at Sinai, the Mount of Obedience, to which it has not yet come; but in the Wilderness, between them.

Look again, without, at the social life, and see how Freedom is invading, wantonly, ruthlessly, some of the sacredest precincts of human life on earth, bringing out and holding up to a cold, critical, public gaze, through the medium of the public press, the private sanctities of the home. See how Freedom to-day is severing some of the sacredest ties of human life on earth, breaking down the home, making the union of those who have been joined together for better or for worse, not an inviolable union with one man and one woman true till death to one another, but a union at convenience, a union simply at pleasure, and while it pleases, and then not a union.

You tell me that these are but tendencies. Yes, but they *are* tendencies in modern life. We note them and we feel them a little. And other tendencies, too, there are, toward wild and excessive freedom, in the same direction working!

Well, what then? Are we discouraged? Is the outlook black and despairing? No. It is bright and inspiring. From Egypt, to the Wilderness, and then to Sinai: from Bondage, to Freedom, and then to Obedience. That is the Divine method of development. Those are the three stages in it. We have passed the first; we have reached the second; we are on our way to reach at last the third. It is the only way in which it can be reached. We cannot go at once from Bondage to Obedience. We can only go from Bondage, through Freedom, to Obedience.

We see that sometimes strikingly illustrated in the individual life; in the case of a young man. He has reached his majority; he is free; free from the bondage of his father's house, of his father's rule and direction. He goes out into the Wilderness, free! And O, how he feels and enjoys his freedom; how he plays with it, and sports with it, wandering in the Wilderness where and as he pleases; sometimes wandering with wild excesses in it! He is on his way to Obedience. Do not worry about him, father and mother; do not break your heart over him. He will reach it; sooner or later he will reach his father's house again; not perhaps to be again an actual dweller in it; but the counsels, the wisdoms, the rules of his father's house;—he will see them, he will understand them, he will appreciate them, he will take them to himself as he never did in his youth, and as when it was or seemed to be a house of bondage to him. Not only to his earthly father's house will he come, but to his heavenly Father's house, to Sinai, the Mount of God, Obedience;—through the Wilderness!

What we see sometimes so strikingly illustrated in one individual, in a broad and general way we see in all life, social, and national, the world life. The qualities that are in it, the forces, faculties, tendencies, which in the house of bondage were hidden and latent in it, must be brought out and freed first in order thus to be redeemed at last and tamed.

If, my friends, we see such forces coming so freely out, sometimes so excessively and so wildly out, in human life to-day, that is what they are coming out for—to be redeemed, all of them; in order that the whole of human life—not a part of it, not a little of it, but the whole of it—and everything that is in it, every force, every passion, may be at last redeemed.

Then give the people freedom; freedom to think, freedom to vote, freedom to live. They may at times, they certainly will, misuse it and abuse it, going wrong with it, going wild with it, going drunk with it! Yet, give the people freedom and never despair. It is the Divine method of development—from Egypt to the Wilderness, and then to Sinai: to Sinai through the Wilderness.

That is the great lesson which in and through and by means of their freedom the people to-day must learn—Obedience, obedience to those great words of God, which, through a Prophet greater than Moses, and on a holier mountain than Sinai, He has spoken to the world. It is the lesson which all of us must try to learn. The wildness that is in us—and there is a wildness in us—we must learn to tame, and we shall learn to tame it, through the experiences and the disciplines and the disillusionments of the Wilderness; we shall learn to tame it. We shall be made to learn that life means, that faith means, that religion means, not bondage and not freedom, but OBEDIENCE, to Jesus Christ.

And far beyond ourselves perhaps will that obedience go; for the fight here in the Wilderness in which we are engaged, as Professor James of Harvard says, seems to be not merely a fight for ourselves, but for the universe as well; as though there were something really *wild* in the universe which we, by our idealities and faithfulnesses and obediences, are needed to redeem."

So it sometimes seems; so it sometimes feels; a fight here in the Wilderness, whose successes of obedience, reach to other spheres beyond us, working out some redemption there, which we when there shall know! The glory there, the far illuminating glory of obedience here! The dominion there, the far extending dominion of obedience here; the redemption there, the far reaching redemption of obedience here, which here and now we give to those great, commanding words of God, spoken through Jesus Christ to the world.

THE SELF-REVEALING VISION.

Nathan said to David, Thou art the man.—2 SAMUEL xii. 7.

THE SELF-REVEALING VISION.

The incident to which these words belong, as related at length in the chapter from which the text is taken, you are doubtless familiar with; for it is a familiar Bible story, and except with the briefest reference I need not recall it to you. David has done a mean, wicked and cruel thing. But he is not aware of it, or he does not seem to be aware of it, or to have within himself any consciousness of the wrong. So that when the prophet comes to him and tells him the story of another man apparently, whose conduct was characterized by the same kind of meanness, by the same kind of baseness, David's anger is greatly kindled against the man; he is full of indignation, of righteous indignation, and he said to Nathan, "As the Lord liveth, the man that hath done this thing shall surely die!" And Nathan said to David, "Thou art the man!"

Self-deception: that is what for a little while this morning I want to talk about.

The faculty of the human heart for the exercise of self-deception is something wonderful, or would indeed be wonderful if it were not so commonly exercised, and in so many ways so often made to appear. The preacher goes up into the pulpit some Sunday morning and preaches his sermon to you; in the course of which he describes not sin in general, nor the exceeding sinfulness of sin, but some particular sin, some particular fault, some moral taint and blemish, some moral defect and weakness, in character or in conduct. And to what he says you listen, with an attentive and intelligent listening. But you seem this morning to be a little more eagerly and keenly attentive than usual; for there is a man here this morning, an acquaintance of yours, a friend. He does not come very often, but he happens to be here this morning; he happens now to be here, whom the preacher seems to describe, to characterize and portray. How fortunate it is, how providential, that he should be here; this day of all days, this man of all men! Yes, he is here; the probability is that he came in when you came in; that he walked up the aisle when you walked up the aisle; that he sat down and took his seat when you sat down and took your seat; that he will go out again when you go out again; you will lodge with him, to-day, to-night, to-morrow, and the day after. And yet, although you will lodge with him, and live with him, and walk about the streets with him, and can never shake him off, you don't know him; for it is you! And *you;* you don't know *you;* you don't see *you!* It is just as difficult to do it with the moral eye as it is with the physical eye. You see only a part of you, and not the most responsible part; the brain, the head, the intelligence, where the responsibility lies. It is the other man you see; his sin, his weakness, his inconsistency, in all its blackness and inexcusableness. But your sin, and your fault, and your inconsistency—you don't see that! You think you do; you say you do; but I am not sure that you do. Or if you do, you see it as something else or less than what it really is; less heinous, less culpable, less reprehensible. You give it another name, a more euphemistic name; you put a mask upon it, palliating it by heredity, extenuating it by circumstance, mitigating it by both, circumstance and heredity, temperament and temptation. You put a mask upon it; in one way or another you deceive—what a strange, psychological process it is—*you deceive yourself about it!*

That is what makes all your Bible reading, and has made it all these years from your youth up until now,—or let me say rather, putting myself in the same condemnation with you,—that is what has made all *our* Bible reading, from our youth up until now, such ineffective reading; not taking it to ourselves, nor applying it to ourselves, who are not in the Bible story, or who do not seem to be in the Bible story, but only to those who are in the Bible story; the baseness of David to David; the cowardice of Peter to Peter; the treachery of Judas to Judas: "As the Lord liveth, the man that did that thing ought to die!" we say. And where is that man? Does he live in Jerusalem or New York? And the formalism that is in the Bible described, and the hypocrisy there portrayed, and the worldliness there denounced, and the covetousness called idolatry which is there condemned—we read it there, we find it there, we see it there, in the Bible; and *we keep it there*, in the Bible; shut up and closed between the Bible covers; not as the mirror of us, revealing and showing us, our formalism and our hypocrisy and our covetousness and our double-dealing, and our inconsistency, and our serving of God and Mammon; but as the mirror of them, of whom the Bible speaks, revealing and showing them, and their formalism and inconsistency and double-dealing.

And so again in our Bible reading, as in our sermon hearing, we try to deceive ourselves; sometimes by the very process of reading the Bible, thinking that thereby we are somewhat better, we try to deceive ourselves. And strange as it seems, inexplicable, theoretically impossible, we *do* deceive ourselves. It is one of those deep, subtle, mysterious functionings of the human heart, or the human soul, or the human something in us, which we do not quite understand. To deceive others about ourselves, or to try at least to do so and in a measure to succeed; that of course we can quite readily understand. But to deceive ourselves, about ourselves; not only to want to do it, and to try to do it, but to *do* it—that is a kind of deception which seems to me to be, something not quite human, something more than human, or something else than human; something ultra-human; disposing us to believe, as we reflect upon it, that each of us is or has two personalities in him, and that one of them is that exceedingly cunning, crafty, intellectually blinding, darkening, bewildering, sophisticating personality that the Bible calls the "Devil"! But whencesoever it comes, or whencesoever it is, it is; that curious force and power, that curious something in us, human or ultra-human, whose tendency is to make us, from ourselves hide ourselves, to ourselves deceive ourselves, and not to know ourselves!

To fight against that tendency, to conquer and overcome it, is the hardest task that human nature can perform. With a confession of sin not too general, not too extravagant either, not too violently denunciatory, which shows that the self-deceiving or the self-excusing is still working in us a little; but with a confession of sin, honest, fair, candid, *our* sin, our besetting sin, our worldliness, our miserliness, our sensuousness; calling it by its right name, seeing it as it is, with no attempt to condone it,—no task I say is harder to perform than that. And yet, my Christian friends, if there is truth in the Christian religion, if there is any truth in the Bible, if there is any truth in the moral nature of man, if there is any moral truth and equity in this universe, it is a task that will some day be performed by us, or for us! And the man who for a time has been deceiving himself about himself, through some prophetic voice sounding in his soul, will at last be undeceived.

In different ways it speaks, that prophetic voice, with different forms of speech. Sometimes it speaks through publicity, to a man; when some sinful thing which he himself has done, some sinful deed or act, some sinful habit, passion, indulgence, which he perhaps in others has so often censured, so often blamed and condemned, not seeing it in himself, not knowing it in himself, concealing it from himself— not only from the world but also from himself—is by the world discovered, or almost discovered. It begins to come out into discovery, it begins to come out into publicity, he begins to fear and tremble that it will come out, for he begins now to see it as it is: the self-deceiving mask which he has put upon it begins now to fall; he begins to see it as it is, as he never saw it before! And O, the horror of it! the shame of it! the guilt of it; the baseness of it; the meanness of it—the right name of it at last!

It sometimes takes publicity to touch and reach the conscience and to make the conscience work. And sometimes, too, it does so work, my friends. We have seen it working so, sounding with prophetic voice in the human soul, and speaking and saying there, "The man whose sin thou hast rebuked, censured and condemned; *thou* art the man!" And as though some great light, fierce and strong, beating down upon him from the throne of God, had pierced his self-deceiving, self-excusing mask; he is made at last to see himself, to know and judge himself!

It sometimes speaks, that prophetic voice, through publicity. It seems to be the only way in which it can speak effectively to some men. To most of us, I presume, who are here this morning, in another way it speaks; not with some loud, harsh, strident, condemning voice without, but in some soft, still, low and appealing voice within. There comes a time when Jesus of Nazareth seems to be passing by; the wonderful Jesus of Nazareth of Whom we learned in childhood, of Whom we have often heard, of Whom we have often read; not only in the Bible but in other books as well; and yet Who, in spite of all our efforts to be a Christian, has seemed so far away, so distant, so remote, like some great character in history; but now, somehow, somewhy, we know not how or why, He seems to be coming our way! He is passing by; His presence we seem to feel touching us, His voice we seem to hear calling us, something seems to be happening to us; something *is;* our blindness is falling away, blindness to ourselves; the worldly film before our eyes is falling now away; our self-deceiving falseness is falling now away; and in that self-revealing light, seeing what we are, we see more clearly Jesus Christ and the way in which through Him to become what we ought to be.

That is the voice pleading with men, entreating men, inviting men, so often heard, and which perhaps is speaking now to you; not to some man somewhere, you don't know where; some vague, indefinite, nondescript, abstract kind of man, like humanity in general. No; he is speaking to *a* man, pleading, inviting, entreating. Where is he? Not a man who stayed at home this morning, but a man who came out this morning—Thou art the man! Jesus Christ wants you, needs you; you need Jesus Christ, to show you what you are, what you ought to do, what you ought to be; to help you to do it, to be it, to live it; a brighter, gladder, purer, stronger, and braver life! speaking now to you and saying, "Thou art the man!"

THE SELF-EVIDENCING VISIONS.

Some mocked; and others said, We will hear thee again of this matter.—THE ACTS xvii. 32.

THE SELF-EVIDENCING VISIONS.

THAT was the effect produced upon his audience by the preaching of Saint Paul at Athens. Not unlike that is the effect which the preaching of the Christian faith has elsewhere produced. It has not always received unanimous assent, but only partial assent; and while it has appealed to some it has not appealed to others; not of necessity because it is different, in different times and places, but because *they* are different, and do not have within them, or do not feel within them, in the same measure, in the same degree of activity, that need of the Christian faith which responds to the Christian faith, and which constitutes one of the strongest vouchers of the Christian faith.

And that is the subject, or that suggests the subject, to which I ask your attention, namely: The Christian Evidences in us; or, Finding in Ourselves the Proof of the Christian Faith.

In one of his interesting essays, Professor James of Harvard compares the world or the government of the world to a lock; and, in order that we may ascertain what kind of a lock it is, moral or unmoral, Nature, he says, has put into our hands two keys. If we try the moral key and *it* fits, it is a moral lock. If we try the unmoral key and *it* fits, it is an unmoral lock, or an unmoral world. And that is good evidence, and the best we can have, of what the world is.

Now, the same simile may be used, not only with reference to the world, but with reference as well to the people in the world. They, too, may be likened to locks. Some keys fit them, and some do not; and the keys which fit some of them do not fit others of them. For there are in the world all sorts of people, with different structural complexities and temperamental arrangements and adjustments and combinations, requiring different keys to open and unlock them. The key that fits the grown-up man, that opens him, to which he responds, does not fit the child. It may be in itself a very good key; or, dropping the simile, it may be in itself a very good thing, wise and right and true; but the child does not perceive it; he cannot perceive it because he is a child; and if when he hears it he does not mock and deride it, he does not very much desire to hear it again.

And the case of the child with reference to the man is the case of the man himself with reference to other men. What seems right and true to the man who is a scholar, with his scholarly tastes and instincts; to the man who is not a scholar does not seem right or true, but foolish perhaps, and wrong. As the remark or the sentiment attributed to the late Professor Agassiz, might seem to some of us— that he had no time to make money. No time to make money! How silly; how absurd! Some mock. Others there are of us perhaps to whom that sentiment appeals. It fits us; it suits us; we respond to it, and are moved perhaps to say, as we hear it by some setter-forth declared, "That is good; that is right; that is true; there is something more worth while to which to give our time than simply the making of money. There is something in that; we will hear thee again of this matter."

So in regard to other sentiments, other ideals in life, or other ideals of life. If they appeal to us, we think them right and true. If they do not appeal to us, we do not think them right and true. And the proof of what they are is not in them, but in us. We are the proof, than which there is for us no more convincing proof.

Something like that is what I mean by finding in ourselves the proof of the Christian faith, or by not finding in ourselves perhaps the proof of the Christian faith. For, with reference to the Christian faith, there are, and there always have been, two classes of persons. Some there are to whom it does not seem to appeal. They are not the kind of persons whom it seems to suit. The key of the Christian faith does not fit them; and no amount of proof, however good and strong, is strong enough to prove it; for there is no proof in them, no intrinsic proof for the extrinsic proof to touch and take hold of and grapple with and bring out, into the validating consciousness of a self-evidencing conviction.

There are such persons in the world. There always have been. It is a type; existing at Athens long ago, existing now in New York. A certain type of person, or a certain kind of person, not of necessity bad, nor unscrupulous, nor uncultivated; often quite the reverse, agreeable, companionable, intelligent. But he does not seem to have the religious instinct in him, or in whom it has not yet appeared, or in whom perhaps it has been crowded out by other things and interests, worldly things and interests, worldly immersions and absorptions, so that he has become in consequence worldly through and through, from surface down to centre and out to surface again. Whose maxims are worldly maxims, whose standards are worldly standards; secularized, materialized, and sometimes—not in his moral principles but in his sensibilities—vulgarized a little; with no longing in him, no aspiration in him toward some ideal life, toward that ideal life which in Jesus Christ the Christian faith presents. He does not feel it; he does not have it; he does not know what it means. When we try to press that Christian faith upon him it has often seemed to produce, as of a key in a lock which it does not fit, a harsh and grating sound, not altogether unlike a scornful mockery in him! Keep it out of his way, and he has nothing to say about it, and is simply indifferent to it; but press it home, and then—that is something for priests and old women and little children, not for me—a scornful mockery in him!

That was one of the effects produced by the preaching of Saint Paul at Athens. "Some mocked; others said, We will hear thee again of this matter." That, too, is one of the effects which the preaching of the Christian faith has since produced. How has it produced it? Not chiefly by an argument, learned and labored, trying thus to prove to men that the Christian faith is true; but simply by the Christian faith itself, stating it, preaching it. Men they were, to whom it seemed at once to appeal; who, when they heard it, were moved to say, "That is good; that is right; that is true. It fits us, it suits us, it is just the thing we need to explain us, to reveal us, to fulfil us; There is something in that; we will hear thee again of this matter." And so they did.

So it was at the first, when the Christian faith was preached. So it has been since when the Christian faith has been preached. It is that which has kept the Christian faith alive, and the preaching of it alive, going on and on, week after week, year after year, century after century, gathering the people together, in congregating assemblies, in temples, in Churches, in great cathedrals, out on the plains, in the open fields, under the open skies. It is that which has kept the Christian faith alive; not controversy, not disputation, for religious controversy, like other controversy, often fails to convince. And the end of a disputation is so often seen to be, not the agreement of the disputants, bringing them closer together, but the *estrangement* of the disputants, putting them farther apart, with each of them more than ever convinced that he alone is right!

No, not by controversy, not by argument, did the Christian faith prove itself to those who heard it first, or to those who have heard it since. It had, and it has, better proof than that. Men heard it, and men hear it, because it seems so well, so admirably to fit them, to explain them, to bring to light the hidden things of darkness in them, to make things in them clear which are not clear without it; proving itself to be true by finding its proof in them, than which there is no better, or more convincing proof, or, if you please to call it so, more scientific proof! For that is scientific proof—something that explains things not otherwise explainable. That was the way in which—if I may partly borrow here and adapt the phrase of another—that was the way in which a Galileo proved the true motion of the world. That was the way in which a Kepler proved the true attraction of the planets. That was the way in which a Newton proved the true mechanism of the heavens; or a Lyell, the true antiquity of the earth; or a Darwin, the true descent and origin of animals and plants upon it : by a something that explained things not otherwise explainable, and finding its proof in them.

So does the Christian faith prove itself to men,

by explaining things in men, deep, dark, hidden, not otherwise explainable, proving itself to be true by finding its proof in them. And how it does explain them! It was the Christian faith of the Resurrection that Saint Paul had been preaching at Athens, the Christian faith of another life, or rather of the continuance, the uninterrupted, unbroken continuance and going on of this life. And how that does explain us, and what there is within us. Those wonderful and mysterious, yet real yearnings and longings and aspirations in us, after something, we know not what; those visions of the ideal which we cannot reach; and loves, and hopes, and dreams, broken now and thwarted and limited by the earth, yet breaking away and going beyond the earth, and trying by beauty, by art, by speech, by music, by song, to express themselves, yet cannot! They shall at last come out, says the Christian faith, and life shall be fulfilled. Yes, how it explains things, which otherwise have no meaning. How it explains things in human life at large, its incompletenesses, its apparent inequities, its wrongs, its sharp distresses, its pains, its failures, its cruelties, which make us feel at times as we look at them, not only that there is no love and no mercy in the universe, but no justice, no rightcousness, no fair dealing in it. Which make us feel at times, as we look upon them, that this great Power or Being that we call God is not as good as man is, and does not care as much; for it all seems so harsh, so pitiless, so cruel, and we cannot understand it!

Bring in the Christian faith, and we do understand it. The story of human life is not told yet. The picture of human life has not been painted yet. Human life itself is not completed yet. We shall hear again of this matter. For it is not finished yet; it is going on and on, to something else and more, its broken fragments gathered, its broken hopes united; going on and on through the school of God on earth, to its real Commencement time, where it shall begin to be at last itself!

How many things it explains, if we only had time to speak of them, thus proving itself to be true to us, by finding its proof in us.

O, men and women, if there are such here, searching, ever searching, for proof of the Christian faith, "dropping buckets into empty wells, and growing old in drawing nothing up"; still searching, searching and saying, "O, that we knew where we might find it;" come, search for it in human life, and find it in yourselves. Listen to Jesus

Christ; and more and more as you hear Him will you be moved to say, "That is good, that is right, that is true; it is better than we knew, it is truer than we thought; We will hear thee again of this matter!"

THE CRITICAL VISION, AND THE LOVING VISION.

Thomas said, Except I shall see in his hands the print of the nails, and put my finger into the print of the nails, and thrust my hand into his side, I will not believe.—St. JOHN xx. 25.

Then Peter turning about seeth the disciple whom Jesus loved following; which also leaned on his breast at supper. Peter seeing him saith, Lord, and what shall this man do? Jesus saith unto him, If I will that he tarry till I come, what is that to thee? Then went this saying abroad among the brethren, that that disciple should not die.—St. JOHN xxi. 20 and part of the following verses.

THE CRITICAL VISION, AND THE LOVING VISION.

THE apostles of Jesus Christ seem to have been selected by Him, not capriciously and at random, but very carefully, and because they constituted in themselves certain types of character, through which His Gospel message, or through which rather He Himself was to be mediumized and interpreted to the world. Those personal types of character were apparently permanent types of character, existing then and existing now, and representing now, as then, different ways of looking at and approaching Jesus Christ.

Two of those personal and permanent types I will ask you this morning to consider; namely, Saint Thomas, who speaks in the first text, and Saint John, who is spoken of in the second; or the critical spirit and the loving spirit, and what they have to say and teach concerning Jesus Christ, and the value of their testimony.

Criticism has always been a most important function, and the critic a most important functionary in the attempted ascertainment of truth. But, what is criticism? And who is the critic? The word, as you know, literally means separation, discrimination, the taking of things to pieces, thoughts, theories, opinions, or whatsoever other things it is directed toward, searching, sifting, dissecting, taking them to pieces. Criticism, therefore, is essentially a negative function. Yet not on that account any the less important. Sometimes it is necessary to take things to pieces. They have not been put together in the right way. They have been put together in the wrong way, like the blocks in a puzzle, or the letters in a game, which have been so arranged by some unskilful hand that the conclusion which they yield is not a right conclusion, and the answer which they give is not a right answer. When that is the case, then the first thing to do is to separate and take them to pieces, in order to rearrange and put them together again.

Now just that is what the critic does. This block, he says, or this letter, is not in the right place. It does not belong here; therefore I must take it out. By and by I will try to put it somewhere else, where it belongs; but just now and first of all I must take it out. And so he does take it out. Let me illustrate, and show you how it is that the critic proceeds.

In the thirty-sixth chapter of the Book of Genesis we have a long list of names of persons who are said to have been the kings of Edom. Then after reciting the list at length, the writer proceeds to say, "*These are the kings who reigned in the land of Edom before there were any kings over the children of Israel.*" Now, who wrote that? Who was the author of it? Moses; who is generally supposed to be the author of the whole Book of Genesis? Evidently and clearly not; for it must have been written after the children of Israel had kings; otherwise the writer could not have referred to those kings. And the children of Israel did not have any kings until long after the time of Moses; in the time of Saul and David and Solomon, when they were settled in the land Canaan. Therefore, Moses did not write that, so the critic says; it does not belong to the time or the authorship of Moses. Therefore I must take it out; not out of the Bible, but out of the time and authorship of Moses. By and by I will put it somewhere else, where it does belong; but just now and first of all I must take it out. And so he does. And we can see clearly enough, when once he states his case, why he takes it out.

Sometimes, however, he cannot state his case so

that we can see it. Only some one else who is a critic like himself can see it; because his critical faculty, by a long, industrious, studious and scholarly training has become a critical instinct in him, so delicate, so sensitive, so fine, that he can almost feel anything out of place in the Biblical text, an anachronism, an interpolation; he can almost feel it there. And those of us who are not as cultivated as he, who have not been lifted up to the same high pitch of critical skill and ability—and that means the great mass, the great majority of Christian men and women in the world—cannot see or follow his critical methods and processes, and appreciate his critical results and findings. Even when he explains them we cannot always see them, we cannot usually see them; and the reasons which he gives we cannot comprehend, we cannot take them in, with the right emphasis, with the right significance.

He reads in the Book of Isaiah, for instance, with the critical faculty in him. By and by he comes to a passage where he stops, and says, "Isaiah did not write that; some subsequent editor put that in." And we ask him how he knows it, and he says to us in reply, "That is not Isaiah's style; he never uses that kind of an idiom, he never uses that kind of a word, in that form, active or passive; he never uses that kind of an accent, that kind of an inflection." "Does he not?" we say. We did not know it, and we do not know it then, even when he tells it to us, except as he tells it to us. For we have not been living with Isaiah as his close and intimate companion, as he has been living with him, for twenty years perhaps, during his whole adult life, even since he left the university; studying Isaiah, his idoms, his moods, his tenses, his words, his accents, his inflections. We do not know Isaiah. *He* does; there is no one else in all the world whom he knows so well. Then some day when he says something about Isaiah, or Saint Paul, or Saint Peter, or Saint Jude, or some other Biblical writer, which the rest of us have not been in the habit of thinking and believing, we call a meeting, an assembly of the brethren, of the clergymen and the laymen; and they come, from their parishes and their stores, from their missions and their merchandise, to take a vote on a question of scholarship, the most critical kind of scholarship, which only the most critical kind of scholarship is competent to consider, which nevertheless they do consider, and decide by a vote, these missionaries and merchants. And then they tell the man whose words they have condemned, that if he continues to say what he has been saying they will cast him out. And of course he continues to say what he has been saying, for he is a scholar, and he knows it is true. And of course they cast him out!

What a strange proceeding it is; and yet it is a proceeding which has been proceeding all along the whole course of Christian history, and is proceeding somewhat to-day. But it is not a right proceeding; it is a wrong proceeding, it is a foolish proceeding.

No, let criticism go on. It has its work to do. It will not take our Bible away; it will not take our Saviour away. It never has done so. But time and time again, when the Bible had become a sealed book to the people, which they either could not read or did not read, it has given to them its treasures again, and made it a living Book. Time and time again, when the vitalizing power of Jesus Christ had become simply a convention, or a name, and had ceased to be felt by society at large, moving and stirring the world, criticism has given Him back to the people again, and made Him a living Christ.

Therefore, I say, let it go on. And by criticism, I do not mean that ghoulish kind of glee that gloats in denunciation and destruction, hurting people's sensibilities unnecessarily. That is not criticism; that is *vandalism*. By criticism I mean, as Professor Caird observes, that pure, passionate devotion to truth, whose tendency is not to negation merely, stopping and resting there, but through negation to reaffirmation, through destruction to reconstruction; or, in Carlyle's language, Through the everlasting No to the everlasting Yea.

Then let it, I say, go on. By and by the world will gather up its fruits which, like the leaves of the tree of life, will be for the healing of the nations.

But in the meantime, my friends, what are we to do? We are not critics. We cannot climb up to those great heights of criticism; we become dizzy there, and lose our balance. We cannot breathe that rare atmosphere of scholarly criticism; we become bewildered there and lose our senses. We are but the people down on the plains, in the valleys, and very busy people. What shall we do? Is there no guide for us? Surely; and the best. It is the guiding spirit of Love, that intensest of all the passions, yet the purest of all the passions, the fiercest yet the mildest, so gentle yet so strong, so yielding yet so firm, which no obstacle impedes, which no barrier bars, which no fetter binds; leaping across the waters, flashing across the lands to where the loved one is, no matter how far away. Unconditioned by space, it is indeed a spirit; unlimited by time, eternal; unbroken by death, immortal; consuming itself with a longing which, in its finite mould, it knows not how to express, as though it felt the quickening breath of an Infinite Presence in it. Infinite, eternal, immortal; it is, that spirit of Love, it is the spirit of God; and therefore an infallible spirit, the only infallible spirit and oracle in all the world. Whose vision is the clearest, whose judgment is the best, going down into the deepest depths, penetrating into the inmost recesses of the character of the person whom it loves, and thus learning to know him, with a truer knowledge of him than all the critical questioning and cross-questioning and examining can impart. And that is the spirit, infinite, eternal, immortal, infallible, the spirit of Love, the spirit of God, which has, like no other, understood and interpreted Jesus Christ.

Yes, men and women there have been in all ages, in all centuries, a great multitude which no man can number, out of all tribes and kindreds and peoples and tongues, who knew Jesus Christ because they loved Jesus Christ, and then loved Him more because they knew Him better. And thus, hand in hand together joined, in divorceless weddedness, Love and Knowledge have gone, Love helping Knowledge, and Knowledge helping Love.

Then let the critic go on. He has his work to do; searching, sifting, dissecting, taking such things to pieces as ought to be taken to pieces in order to put them back again in better shape and form, and thus like the old voice of John the Baptist, crying in the wilderness, making straight the path that leads to Jesus Christ; then in due season pointing to Him, and saying, "Behold, the Lamb of God!" Yes, let the critic go on with his work, pointing to Jesus Christ. But love is there before him, before the critic comes, and has already beheld Him. For love is strong and quick, and its footsteps are very swift.

That is what, by the Church of God, is needed most to-day. Criticism is needed: love for Jesus Christ, *that* is needed more; not only thus to have a better knowledge of Him, but so thus to give a better service to Him, more willing and more glad, finding His yoke an easy yoke and His burden not hard to bear.

That is the path, my friends, in which we all can walk. It is not in any worldly sense an exalted path; it is a lowly and humble path, in which the lowly and the humble walk, and always have walked. No, it is not an exalted path, but it is a good path, and safe, and leading straight to Jesus Christ. The other path, the path of critical research, is long and tedious and tortuous, and full of difficulty and danger. That too is a good path for those who are competent to walk in it; but it is not the path in all probability for us, though to some of us perhaps it may seem a more appealing and a more attractive path. It seems to take more courage; we like its difficulties; we court its dangers; they seem to give us a pleasing sense of intellectual life, of intellectual activity, of intellectual attainment and achievement. We do not want to go with the great multitudinous mass, with the great majority, on the easy path of love, into the kingdom of God. That will not do for us; that is too sentimental, too weak: too womanish perhaps we call it. We want to go with the cultivated few, with the critics, with the scholars, into the kingdom of God, daring to be singular and alone, even if we never find and reach any kingdom of God.

That voice we hear to-day. All down through the ages we hear it; not the voice of a true scholarship and criticism, but of a pseudo-scholarship and criticism. All down the ages we hear it: in the Apostolic times, in the Apostolic group, following after Jesus Christ, there too perhaps it was heard.

> "Doubting Thomas and loving John,
> Behind the others walking on.
> Tell me now, John, dare you be
> One of the minority?
> To be lonely in your thought,
> Never visited nor sought,
> Shunned with secret shrug; to go
> Through the world esteemed its foe?
> To be singled out and hissed,
> Pointed out as one unblessed,
> Warned against in whispers faint,
> Lest the children catch a taint;
> To bear off your titles well,
> Heretic and Infidel?
> If you dare, come with me,
> Fearless, confident and free.

> "Thomas, do you dare to be
> One of the majority?
> To be only as the rest
> With heavens common comforts blessed?
> To accept in lowly part
> Truth that shines on every heart;
> Never to be set on high
> Where the envious curses fly;
> Never name or fame to find,
> Still outstripped in soul and mind;
> To be hid, unless to God,
> Like one grass blade in the sod,
> Under foot by millions trod?
> If you dare, come with us, be
> Lost in Love's great unity."

Then went the saying abroad, that that disciple should not die. Ah yes, that disciple dies, but not the spirit of love which that disciple embodies. That will still go on and on, brightening, broadening, through the ages, interpreting Christ, revealing Christ, entering into the inmost secrets of Christ, and blessing the world with Christ. That will still live, will linger, will last, will tarry, till He come!

THE VISION OF A SPIRITUAL GUIDE.

Have ye received the Holy Ghost, since ye believed?—THE ACTS xix. 2.

THE VISION OF A SPIRITUAL GUIDE.

SAINT PAUL, in the course of his journeying, comes to the city of Ephesus, and finding there certain persons who professed to be disciples of the new religion, he puts to them the question which I have just repeated, and to which they answer, No; that they had not even heard of a Holy Ghost. We cannot plead their ignorance so far as the name is concerned, but I wonder whether we understand much better than they what that name implies, or the purport of the question with which it is associated. Let us inquire, and in order to do it the better, let us inquire first what it was that distinguished so radically the Jewish religion from the Christian.

It was a characteristic of the Jewish religion that it essayed to govern and control all the actions of men by a series of formal precepts, of formal laws and rules. They started, those Jewish people, upon their national career, with the Commandments given by Moses, which they were enjoined by Moses himself, most carefully and conscientiously to keep. It was soon discovered, however, that there were many forms and phases and varieties of human experience to which those old Mosaic laws did not directly apply. And so it came to pass that those Mosaic laws were supplemented in time with numerous other laws, to enable the people thus to meet their new and changed conditions, until at last they became, those supplemental laws, so voluminous and vast, that they extended to and covered all the minutest features and details of their life. And everything they did was done by some religious rule; and without some religious rule was not anything done that was done. And yet, and this is the point that I want you to observe, it was these most devout, conscientious and religious people, with a pious phrase for every act and almost every thought, who always had their rules, their religious rules at hand, to tell them how to eat and drink and talk and walk and work and play, as well as how to pray, with a moral casuistry that has never been surpassed; it was these most conscientious and religious people who have gone upon the record as having committed the most diabolical act of wickedness in the history of mankind. Who not only failed to recognize a beautiful moral brightness, an ideal moral goodness, when it appeared before them, but called it darkness and evil, and became so incensed with Jesus Christ, Who revealed it, that they put Him to a criminal's death and cast Him out of the world! And why did they do it? Because they were conscienceless, and vicious and irreligious, above all other peoples? No, they were conscientious and religious; they were very conscientious and religious. Why then did they do it? Simply because they had become so dependent upon formal laws and rules in the regulation of their conduct, and in the formation of their judgments, that when they were brought face to face with such a new, original type of goodness, as they had never seen before; not having any *rule* at hand with which to measure and appraise it, they could not understand it, they did not know what to do with it; and the only thing they could do with it was to do with it what they did with it, and that was to reject it!

This, is the lesson by their experience taught, for that age and people, for this age and people, for every age and people, that human life cannot be always guided toward what is right and true and good by precepts and rules; that there is no moral casuistry, no moral code or book, no moral pharmacopœia, no matter how elaborate and large, to which we can always go, and in which we can always find such ready-made prescription or counsel or direction as we at times require. Difficulties will arise, perplexities will appear, situations will ensue, entanglements will come, weaving themselves around us, with something new and strange and unfamiliar in them, and not like anything else, either in our own experience or in the experience of others. Have you not found it so? Have you not found yourselves so circumstanced at times that nothing you could think of in all your past experience, or in anybody's past experience, seemed just exactly to meet your case? It seemed a peculiar case. It was. Not in all respects but in some; and it was just there that it seemed so hard and perplexing, in those some respects which differentiated your case and situation from every other case, which made it so unique, without parallel, without precedent to fall back upon, to guide you, to help you, to make you see and know what you ought to do, and give you strength to do it.

Surely you have found it so. We have all found it so. It is human life, which seems to have an infinite quantity in it, an infinite potentiality of variety in it; which therefore into new conditions is always coming out, into new conditions growing, making every day a new day, with some new features in it; making every age a new age with some factors in it, and which in some new manner every day and every age and every person in it must sooner or later meet.

What therefore is needed, for the guidance of our life, for the guidance of the world, is not a law old or new, however good, nor a lawgiver, however wise, but something else than a law, something more than a lawgiver, something that can enter easily, like an atmosphere, like a current of air, like a wind, into all those new conditions which our human life is forever taking on.

That is what is needed. That is what the Founder of the Christian religion gives. Not what the founder of the Jewish religion gives—a law, a rule, a decalogue, a statute, a code, a book. For whether or not it be true that Moses wrote the Pentateuch, it certainly is true that Jesus Christ wrote nothing, absolutely nothing, except when upon one occasion, He stooped down, and with His finger wrote on the ground, and it was soon obliterated and lost; and no man knows what He wrote. Not a single word of any sort, on paper or on parchment, has He left behind. What then does He leave behind? Or what does He say He will leave, as to his people on the earth His last and greatest bequest? What is that bequest? A breath, a spirit, a ghost. That is all. That is all He said they would receive. And so they did receive it, when, with one accord, they were all assembled in one place, and suddenly there came a sound as of a rushing mighty wind, like some impalpable presence, like some intangible force; and they were filled with the Holy Ghost! It was the birthday of the Christian religion and its career upon the earth, or of the Christian Church and its history in the world. And then those representatives of the Christian Church on earth, feeling that influence in them, that Breath, that Spirit, that Ghost, that rushing mighty wind entering into their hearts, into their lives, taking possession of them; then did they begin to feel as they had never felt before, to know, to believe, as they had never believed before. Then did they begin to speak with new tongues, that they had never spoken before. Then power came upon them, not only to make them see and know what they ought to do, but to give them strength to do it.

That was the bequest which Jesus Christ bequeathed. That was what He gave. That was what He left,—a Spirit, a Breath, a Ghost, a Holy Ghost. When therefore Saint Paul comes to the city of Ephesus, and finds certain persons there who profess to be disciples of the new religion, he very naturally wants to know whether they had come into this great spiritual bequest. They believed in Jesus Christ, so it appears, and what they had heard about Him, His birth, and life and death, His wonderful victory over death. Yes, orthodox and sound in the faith, they believed in Jesus Christ. But that was not the point. "Have you received the Holy Ghost since you believed?" And they scarcely knew what He was talking about; they scarcely knew what He meant.

Well, do we know what he meant? What is our guide in life? A holy Spirit, or a holy Book? This Book, this Bible? I speak to those to-day who sincerely and profoundly reverence this Book. I share that reverence with them. And the more I search and study and look into its pages, the more that reverence grows. This strange and wonderful Book, which although it has been so frequently attacked, and so fiercely, too, attacked, has never been destroyed; of which it has been said that, like a cube of granite, no matter how often you overturn it, it is always right side up. This strange and wonderful Book, of which the strange and eccentric Rousseau, has said, that one only needs to read it, in order to feel for a moment at least the impulse to obey it. Of which the ecclesiastic Cardinal Newman has said, that in spite of all the exploring with which it has been explored, it has not yet been explored, but has in it heights and depths unscaled and unfathomed, and fertile glades, and beautiful streams whose source has not been reached, and which is always full of fresh surprises for us. Of which the great Oriental scholar, Sir William Jones, so familiar with the literature of the world has said, that it contains a greater sublimity, a purer morality, a nobler type of life, a clearer spiritual vision, sweeter strains of music, of poetry, of passion, of eloquence, than could be brought together within the same enclosure from all the books of every sort that have ever been composed in any tongue or speech.

But time would fail me to tell—the libraries are full of them—of all the various tributes, by all sorts and conditions of men, rendered to this book, which has been, which is, which will be, I think, forever inseparably intertwined and associated with the destinies of mankind.

And yet, my friends, it is not chiefly the Book that is our guide in life, but the spirit rather which inspired those who wrote the Book; which, beneath its surface forms of limited human judgment, of partial human thought, of imperfect human speech, from first to last pervades it. That is our guide— not first of all the Book, but first of all the Spirit. Without that Spirit in us we cannot hope to know and understand the Book. Without that Spirit in us its light will be to us, as it has so often been to others, a light to lead astray. We will not only fail to perceive the marvelous unity of the Book, but will somehow be able to prove, by quoting its statements here and there, whatever we wish to prove. Hence to you and me the pertinency of the question which in the text is found. You believe, you say, the Bible; you reverence, you admire it, you sing and sound its praises. You Protestant men and women, you particularly, you believe in the Bible, the heritage of your home, taught you by father and mother, consecrated by their prayers. You have always believed in the Bible. That is right and good. Have you received the Holy Ghost since you believed, to help you now to read the Book, to understand the Book, to enjoy the Book; have you received the Holy Ghost since you believed?

That is the guide which Jesus Christ has left, which Jesus Christ has given, as His great and last bequest; for the writing of the Book which has been by others written; and for the writing of the book which we ourselves are writing, the Book of Human Life, and in which day after day we are writing something,—the way in which we do our work in life, encounter its duties, its difficulties, its dangers, so often strange and new, confusing and bewildering, without any precedent to help us, to enable us to meet them. And how can we meet them? We have our Christian creeds, our Christian rules and laws, which we regard as right, which we regard as true, and in which we believe. But sometimes, as you know, those Christian creeds and doctrines do not seem to touch and cover all our case, our actual situation, with all the features in it. And something else we need, something more we need, not simply something to believe, but something to inspire, an inspiration we need which is also good and true,—a Breath, a Spirit, a Ghost, a Holy Ghost, to purify the heart, of all the baser thought and baser feeling in it, and to make it thus a medium for apprehending God; to clarify the vision, and thus to cause us to know, as by a kind of instinct in us, what we ought to do; to make us quick to see, strong to act, steadfast to endure, and to our human life to give its highest pitch of power: an inspiration in us, a Holy Ghost in us.

That is what is needed. Hence again the pertinency to you and me of the question which in the text is found. We are talking so much to-day about our creeds and doctrines, we are trying to ascertain what we think is right and what we think is true, what we ought to believe and what we do believe. Well, that is good. But there is something else;—have we received the Holy Ghost since we believed, to make our belief alive and like an inspiration to sing its song within us? That is what is needed. By the world at large it is needed, to exalt it, to ennoble it, to give it a great and worthy and Divine enthusiasm. By the Christian Church it is needed to quicken and arouse it, to make it do again upon the earth an Apostolic work, to send it forth, not grudgingly, or of necessity, but with gladness and joy, with an inspiration in its heart to conquer the world for Christ, " Beautiful as Tirzah, comely as Jerusalem, terrible as an army with banners."

That is what every one of us needs,—a Breath, a Spirit, a Ghost, a Holy Ghost, to help us, to guide us, to be the common guide of all of us, entering into the life of all of us; near to me in my life, and yet as near to you, with those on sea and land; thus guiding our life on earth, through tempest and through storm, through tumult and through strife, through all the wild confusion of tongues, until we come at last to the haven where we would be!

"Have you received the Holy Ghost?"

THE VISION OF DEATH.

Man goeth to his long home, and the mourners go about the streets.—ECCLESIASTES xii. 5.

To die is gain.—PHILIPPIANS i. 21.

THE VISION OF DEATH.

HERE are two views of death. The first is very mournful and pessimistic, and regards death as a loss. The second is very hopeful and optimistic, and regards death as a gain. Which is the better and truer view? As far as it is possible to do so, within the limitations of a sermon, let us try to ascertain.

And first, putting aside the Bible for a while, let us see what the book of Nature says, as some of its best interpreters to-day are telling us how to read it.

This physical world is alive, so these teachers tell us; not only has life in it, but is itself alive, with nothing in it dead, nor even indeed asleep, with everything in it awake, very wide awake, always wide awake, never sleeping, never at least resting. No matter how fixed and still it seems, it is neither fixed nor still. Some living force is in it, pervading it, controlling it, giving motion to it, a constant motion to it, of energy and life. "If," says the author of Cosmos, "we imagine in a vision of fancy, the acuteness of our senses preternaturally sharpened and quickened, even to the extremest limits of telescopic vision, and incidents whose happenings are now so far apart, divided by long, vast intervals of time, compressed into a single day or into a single hour, everything like rest, in all spatial existence, will forthwith disappear." We shall find that the innumerable groups of fixed stars are not fixed, but moving, and always moving, and everything in them moving, and never ceasing to move, with energy and life. Corresponding to this is the testimony of another eminent naturalist, Professor Huxley, when, in a well-known passage, he says, "The wonderful noonday silence of a tropical forest is after all due to the dulness of our hearing. If our ears could only catch the murmurs of those tiny maelstroms, as they whirl in the innumerable myriads of living cells that constitute each tree, we should be stunned as with the roar of a great city."

Yes, everything is in motion, with energy and life, from a molecule to a mountain, made up of molecules; from a particle to a planet, of particles composed; from a sand grain on the earth to the stars that shine above it; some force of life is in it, some force of life pervades it. The power of life it shows, the presence of life it feels, the song of life it sings, or the psalm of life it sings, like some great hymn of praise, which, in all its vibrant tones, its great Composer hears.

That is one thing which that we are beginning to learn to-day from the study of the book of Nature —that the universe is alive. Something else we are learning. That something else is this: that the life which the universe has, that the life which the universe is, has been from the very beginning a steadily growing life, going on and on, from lower forms to higher, and higher and higher still, not only always moving, but always moving *up*, reaching out to be expressed in some more vital life.

What is the vitalizing principle of this vitalized universe? What is it that has made it vital? What is it that, in other words, has given to it life? Death has given to it life; or Death at least has made its life a steadily growing life, an ever-increasing life, lifting it up and on to higher life and larger and richer and fuller life. The lower form is sacrificed and dies and disappears; then, only then, the higher form appears,—through death. Death is but the gate, the open gate, through which the life can pass, and must pass, in order to reach and find and enter upon its more abundant life. Death, therefore—so we are learning to-day from the naturalistic creed—death is not the foe of life, it is the friend of life, in friendly alliance with it, giving to it friendly aid, friendly succor and help. Yes, more than that; Death is the *mother* of life, bringing it forth as her child, never forsaking her child, and causing her child to live a more abundant life.

I know that that is not the way in which we have been in the habit of regarding death. It has generally been supposed that death first came into the world as the consequence of sin. So it *is* the consequence of sin; and the sinner dies, and the saint lives, in him who was a sinner, because the sinner dies. Death is the consequence of sin, the beneficent consequence of sin, thereby giving life. But death did not first come into the world as the consequence of sin. This physical creed declares, and proves with abundant proof, that long before there was any sin or any sinner in the world, death was in the world. And as far as we can see and go, with backward glance and step, in the history of the world's formation, from the very beginning, whenever that beginning was, death has always been in the world, as the handmaid of life, ministering unto life; not cursing life but blessing life, not hurting life but helping life, causing life to grow, by taking out of its way whatever stunted its growth, whatever hindered its growth, until at last, through death, removing more and more from this growing life, the things that held it back, this growing life was made to grow into our human life.

So the naturalistic or physical creed declares. Without the previous working in the world of death, there would have been, there could have been, no human life at all. We are indebted for it to death. Death is the mother of life.

That is what, concerning death, the book of Nature is teaching us to-day. Or, reverting to our simile, and regarding Nature herself as some great psalm of life, some great hymn of praise, sounding and singing forever in the Almighty's ear, this is the one refrain sounding through it all, and which in all we hear, "To die is gain." "To die is gain." Mingling with its deeper notes, its harsher strident tones, its more complicated harmonies, and seeming again to pervade them all and to repeat its echoed refrain "To die is gain; is Gain, is GAIN; and LIFE is what it gains!"

That is what the naturalistic scriptures are teaching us and that is what precisely the Christian scriptures are teaching, and have long taught, that the greatest friend of the human kind, of the human race, is Death, giving to it life, larger life, higher life, more abundant life. That is why in the Christian scriptures we read so much about the cross, as the sign or the symbol of death; and are so often urged to take and bear the cross, as the sign and symbol of death, and thus through death to live. For that is the way to live, the Christian creed declares, as the naturalistic creed; that is the way to live. Some of us perhaps have not learned that creed yet. We cannot say it, we cannot recite it, we stumble at it, we are offended by it. It seems so harsh and gloomy. Therefore we cannot believe it, and we do not want to believe it. Therefore, when religion comes, and has so much to say about bearing the cross, and making sacrifices, and practising self-denials, and abstaining from this and refraining from that, and foregoing and surrendering and giving up something else; it all seems we think so very unattractive, so sad, so gloomy, so melancholy, like death; and we do not want death, we want life. Of course we do. Everybody wants life. But it is not everybody who has learned that that is the way to get it, and the only way to get it,—that he has to die to get it.

And yet, sooner or later, everybody from his own experience does learn it. And the life which tries to live without dying, dies. I do not mean merely that it comes by and by to the end of its earthly existence, and dies, but that during its earthly existence it dies, fades, withers, dies out. Its pleasures cease to please, or cease to please so much. By and by they cease to please at all; there is no pleasure in them; it dies out. Continuous indulgence has killed it. It is Nature's law of reprisal. Or it is God's law of reprisal, and beneficent reprisal; making the life that tries to live without dying, die; that so perhaps at last, having tasted in its own experience death, it may try to begin to live.

But in some way sooner or later we find that death is not an enemy, but only an enemy in appearance, and not in fact an enemy. Death in fact is a friend of life, healing life and helping life and giving renewal to life, and in many beneficent ways ministering unto life.

I know of course what possibly has been in the minds of some of you, that the Bible speaks of Death as an enemy, and that we have been in the habit of calling it an enemy. Saint Paul so speaks of and calls it when he says, " The last enemy that shall be destroyed is Death." But how is an enemy to be destroyed? How is your enemy to be destroyed? By always fighting and contending with him, and trying in that way to get the victory over him? Well, that is one way. But it is not the only way, nor the most effectual way. For even when your enemy is thus destroyed and crushed, he is still your enemy and would hurt you if he could. There is another way. There is such a thing as arbitration, some one coming between you and your enemy, settling claims, adjusting differences, removing misunderstandings, thus destroying your enemy by destroying his enmity toward you, or your enmity toward him; thus making your enemy your friend. Have you not sometimes found it so in your own experience, that some of your bitterest foes in life have come to be through a better understanding, your best and truest friends? That is the way in which Jesus Christ destroys, or helps us to destroy our enemy, coming as it were between us and our enemy Death, as the reconciler, as the arbitrator, arbitrating the differences, removing the misunderstandings, which are altogether upon our part; thus reconciling us to our enemy, making our enemy our friend; showing us, telling us, that he is our friend, or ready to be our friend, our best and truest friend.

Nature herself has been teaching that, and saying, "To die is gain." But the teaching of Nature, while clear enough in a general way, with reference to the gain of the type or the race through death, is not perhaps so clear with reference to the gain of the individual form, the individual life, the personal life through death, but only seems to suggest it. That is where and how the teaching of Jesus Christ completes the teaching of Nature, carrying it up, carrying it on, making it more direct, giving it personal point, saying, " Yes, for you, the individual, in your individual life, To die is gain. Therefore, come, yield, surrender, give yourself to Me, take and bear the cross, follow after Me, learn from the cross, to yourself to die, and thus by dying to yourself to make yourself alive; not thus to lose your life, but thus to win your life, and all the best things in it which it has to give, and what it means and is."

For what is life? Is it peace? Peace: that deep calm of the soul within, when the tempests rage without, which none of the surface storms of earth can go deep enough to touch: Then must we learn to die, to ourselves to die. Take up the cross, says Christ. What is life? Is it courage? There is no high and great life without it; that force which nothing affrights, which goes right on, never turning from its path in the straight line of duty. Then must we learn to die, to ourselves to die. Take up the cross, says Christ. What is life? Is it happiness? Not happiness without trouble and care, there is no such happiness; but happiness in spite of trouble and care, to lighten care, to brighten trouble. Would we have it? Then must we learn to die, to ourselves to die. Take up the cross, says Christ.

What is life? Is it love? Love, with a human sympathy in it, so big, and great, so wide and deep, that on its heart it bears, like Jesus Christ Himself, the burden of human sin and the burden of human sorrow. We need such love in life; then must we learn to die, to ourselves to die. Take up the cross, says Christ, and thus by dying love, and thus by dying live.

That, my friends, is the way in which to look upon death. That at least is the way in which I look upon it. I see it here and now working both in physical nature and in human nature, as the faithful friend of both, wounding and hurting at times as the faithful friend does. And so I think it will at last prove itself to all, as already it has proved itself to some who have gained through death while here a more abundant life. So has it proved itself to some who are not here, but who have gained through death, somewhere else than here, a more abundant life. So I think it will at last prove itself to all, a true and faithful friend. "The mourners go about the streets, for man goeth to his long home." Is that death? Is that the end of it? No, says the naturalistic creed: no says the Gospel creed: no says Jesus Christ. "To die is gain," and what it gains is Life!

THE VISION OF LIFE.

Ye shall know that I am the Lord, when I have opened your graves.—EZEKIEL xxxvii. 13.

THE VISION OF LIFE.

In the chapter from which the text is taken, the prophet sees the vision of dead men raised to life. The dead men whom he sees are the children of Israel themselves, who at that particular time are scattered in foreign lands, fugitives and outcasts, discouraged and disheartened, without hope, without faith, without God, without life, dead, morally and spiritually dead, and in their graves. That was then their condition, their moral and spiritual condition, so the prophet declares. What therefore they needed was what the prophet said they would some day experience. And speaking in the name of Him Whose messenger he was, he says, "I will open your graves; I will cause you to come up out of your graves, and ye shall know that I am the Lord, when I have opened your graves."

Let us take these words this Easter Day and find in them our theme—a Risen Life as a Testimony to a Risen Lord.

Among the multitude of the figures on the walls of the Sistine Chapel in the Vatican Palace at

Rome, there is one which, according to the English art critic, Mr. Addington Symonds, was intended by its artist to symbolize the spirit of the Italian Renaissance. It is, he says, the figure of a woman rising from the tomb, with the grave clothes still upon her, enshrouding and concealing her eyes, gathered around her breast, encircled about her limbs, and impeding thus somewhat the free movement of her body. Yet she is slowly rising, scarcely conscious and only half awake, struggling with the slumbers and the stupors of death, by the quickening impulse in her of some uplifting power, some resurrecting power, toward some resurrection life, which she has not seen as yet, but which thus she proves to be a resurrection life, veritable and real; because it has opened her grave.

So did Michael Angelo, according to the critic to whom I have referred, symbolize his age. So it seems to me, with equal truth and pertinency, if not indeed with more, might we also symbolize that other great new birth, that other great awakening in the Apostolic age; when all over the Pagan world the spectacle was seen of men and women beginning to rise, coming up out of their tombs, their moral and spiritual tombs, with the grave clothes still upon them of the old Pagan thoughts, the old Pagan customs; yet gradually casting them off, and slowly rising and moving toward, and reaching more and more some higher form of life, more beautiful, more free, some resurrection life. Thus revealing to us in that early, and remarkable Apostolic age, a great moral renaissance, a great moral revival, than which in all the history of the world before there never had been a greater, never one so great; a great moral revival, not sentimental and emotional and passing away, but real, radical, enduring, in conduct, in character, in life, like a beautiful golden morning dawn breaking over the world, and changing the face of the world.

It is a matter of history; you can read it. What brought it about? The preaching of the gospel of a risen Jesus Christ. How? The men and women living then, or the great majority of them, had not seen Him rise; neither had they seen Him after He had risen. How then did they know it? What was their assurance, their evidence, their proof? The testimony of others? That by itself, no matter how clear and strong and indubitable, would not have been enough to persuade and convince them. How then were they persuaded? How then were they convinced? Because the risen Lord, Whom others said they had seen, had proved Himself to be a risen Lord to them. The testimony of others; they had it in themselves, more personal, more direct, and was thus by them confirmed. The fact that He had risen was thus by them attested, was thus by them evinced, because He had opened their graves, their moral and spiritual graves, had brought them out of their graves, and they knew that He was the Lord, the risen Lord, when He had opened their graves. That was the testimony which they had, and which they gave, in that early age; the testimony of a risen life to a risen Lord.

That is the testimony which has been given since by other and later ages, the testimony of a new life coming up out of its grave, its moral and spiritual grave; not all at once and fully, but slowly and gradually, with the grave clothes still wrapped around it, adhering and clinging to it, and thus impeding somewhat its upward movement and course; and sometimes dragging it down and back into its again Pagan grave.

Looking back over the history of the Christian civilization that is what we see, from the beginning until now; a slowly and gradually rising moral and spiritual life, coming up out of its tomb, and then at times dropping back into its old tomb again, its old Pagan tomb, with the old Pagan hardness and Pagan deadness in it. Just as the buried summer beauty, the buried summer bloom in the cold and wintry earth, when touched and quickened by the breath of the resurrecting Spring, begins to rise, not fully, not all at once, but gradually, with the old wintry grave clothes of cold and frost and snow, the wintry winding sheet, the wintry shroud of death, adhering and clinging to it, and wrapping it about: as though for a time there had come winter again. So in the gradual rise and progress of the Christian civilization, every now and then a great outburst of Paganism has appeared, like winter in the spring, with the old Pagan ideas, with the old Pagan passions, thus obscuring, and destroying, or seeming to destroy, the Christian civilization, like the coming back of the old Pagan winter again.

Looking back, I say, over the history of the Christian civilization, something like that is what we see at times. Something like that is what we see in some of the nations now, a great outburst of Paganism in them, with the old Pagan strifes and passions, with the old Pagan ideas of national supremacy and greatness, as though a Christian nation were of the first and highest class—not because it has the highest Christian ideals, toward which its people, rich and poor aspire. No; but simply because it has, the greatest standing armies, the greatest floating navies, the greatest physical equipment, the greatest physical armament, of soldiers and ships and guns.

It sometimes seems, my friends, as though our modern Christian civilization were not Christian at all, as measured by the standard of Him, the story of Whose risen and victorious life created the Christian civilization, and gave the first ennobling and quickening impulse to it; as though, I say, our Christian civilization were not Christian at all, but simply the old Pagan civilization rehabilitated and revived, or with a great deal at least of the old Paganism in it, breaking out in it and seeming to destroy it. Just as the wintry frost, the wintry cold and snow, breaking out in the spring, seems to kill the spring. And yet after all it is not so. No winter's frost ever killed a spring. It may have hindered and delayed it, but it has not killed it, nor prevented the coming out at last of the exuberant summer life in all that varied richness of beauty and of bloom, which, for the assuring of our hearts, we have gathered around us in this Church to-day. And so no outburst of Paganism has ever killed the growing Christian civilization, and it never can or will. Civilization will cast it off, and come up again out of its grave.

For nations, as for individuals, a new and higher Christian life is coming. No winter's frost and snow, no cold Pagan blast, can prevent its coming. It will come; it is coming. The world will rise; it is rising; with the grave clothes about it to be sure of the old Pagan practices, and the old Pagan virtues rather than the Christian virtues; and the old Pagan conformities, and the old Pagan beliefs, or rather the old Pagan unbeliefs, doubts, questions, misgivings, uncertainties; yes, with the grave clothes round about it. Yet it is slowly rising, scarcely conscious and only half awake, struggling with the stupors of death; but it is rising, by the quickening impulse in it of that uplifting power, of that ideal righteousness once seen upon the earth, and of which it is said that death did not destroy it; by the quickening impulse in it of the risen Jesus Christ, ennobling men, purifying men and making them alive, and more and more alive, opening their graves, their moral and spiritual graves, causing them to come up out of their graves. Then will the men of this generation know that He is the Lord, the risen Lord: and doubt and question will go. They will know that He is the Lord, not merely by historical inquiry and research, or philosophic and scientific investigation, but in addition to that—when He has opened their graves.

That is the way in which the Christian world has verified the risen Jesus Christ, and in which it will continue to do so. That is the way, my friends, in which you and I, in our personal lives, can verify the risen Jesus Christ. We do not and cannot see the risen Jesus Christ. Even if we did, if that were the only sign or symbol which we had, it would not be enough, and we would soon somehow persuade ourselves that we had been mistaken in what we thought we saw. Neither would the testimony of others be enough, for we would easily persuade ourselves that they had been mistaken in what they thought they saw. But when, through the power of a faith in the risen Jesus Christ *we* rise, out of our worldliness, our low ideals in life, when *we* rise to a higher and purer life, with higher and purer aims and thoughts and feelings and ambitions, when He has opened our graves, then we shall know that He is the Lord.

Yes, our graves. We have them. The grave in which our personal love lies buried; the love that was on earth our solace and our peace, whose light shone upon our path, to guide us on our way, to sweeten the bitterest cup, to ease the heaviest burden, to brighten the darkest day, but now gone out, and perished, buried in the grave; *our* grave it is. Oh! has it gone forever? Then how harsh, how hard, how cruel, how unfair. But the risen Jesus Christ has given new lease to love, has opened the grave, and we know that He is the Lord. *Our* graves, in which you and I and all of us in a little while shall ourselves be buried, with all our struggling efforts toward righteousness and duty and truth, with all those earnest longings and aspirations in us, which, though limited now by the horizons of the earth, yet seem to be ever struggling toward some risen life above it, some ideal life beyond it, as though they belonged to it; yet mocking us, cheating us and deceiving us, and destined at last to perish. But the risen Jesus Christ has given new lease to life, has opened the grave and shown us that human life goes on. And He is our Lord, because He has given us that everlasting hope.

The graves of our buried ideals, which we older men and women are apt to lose and bury as we get on in life; the graves of our buried experiences, of our buried hopes, of our buried loves and lives, Jesus Christ has opened them. Is not that strong assurance, reasonable assurance that He is the risen Lord? If you please to call it so, is it not philosophic and scientific assurance that He is the risen Lord? Doesn't it work well? Has it not always worked well when it has been allowed to work? Has He not opened the graves, and lifted up human life on earth? Then, fill the Churches to-day with beauty and with bloom; let the arches and the vaults echo and reëcho with the sublimest strains of music, all too inadequate, which the genius of man has inspired; all of them uniting in one great choral voice, and saying and singing this Easter Day, "O, Earth, Earth, Earth, hear the words of the Lord, Who has opened for you your graves!"

THE VISION OF HELL.

If I make my bed in hell, behold, Thou art there!
—PSALM cxxxix. 8.

THE VISION OF HELL.

It is one of the fundamental teachings both of philosophy and theology, not only that God is, but that He is everywhere. No matter where we go, in fact or in fancy, physically or imaginatively, we cannot go from Him. He is immanent in the world, says Philosophy; He is omnipresent, says Theology; the meaning of which the Psalmist has poetically expressed when he says, "Whither shall I flee from Thy spirit? If I take the wings of the morning and remain in the utmost part of the sea, even there Thy hand shall hold me. If I say, peradventure the darkness shall cover me, my night shall be turned into day. If I climb up into heaven Thou art there. If I make my bed in hell, behold, Thou art there!" He seems to exhaust the universe, as he apprehends it, its breadths, and depths, and heights, its darkness and its light, and finds God everywhere, in heaven, and in hell!

I will ask you this morning to consider this last finding of God upon the part of the Psalmist. Putting the matter topically, I will call my subject this, "The Fact and the Fate of Hell."

Clergymen, and others, who are supposed to make a special study of religion, are sometimes asked the question, whether they believe, in these enlightened days, in the existence of a hell. How that question is in all cases answered I do not of course know. I only know how I would answer the question myself, if one should think it worth while to put such a question to me. Without any hesitation I would make reply, "I *do* believe in hell!" And, if I were asked further the reason of my belief, I would make reply again, that "I believe in the existence of a hell because I believe in the existence of a God!"

That may seem at first like a curious, if not an illogical and inconsequential reason. But think a moment. If God is, then righteousness is; and if God is everywhere, then righteousness is everywhere; not indeed of necessity everywhere obeyed, but everywhere prescribed as a law to be obeyed. As the law of physical gravity is everywhere prescribed as a law to be obeyed, so is the law of righteousness everywhere prescribed as a law to be obeyed. If in any case, or in any place, in the universe, this world, or another, that law is disobeyed, sinned against and broken, the consequence is loss, injury, disaster, serious loss and disaster, very serious loss, personal loss and disaster; very personal loss. And that personal loss is hell!

"The sinner," says the Bible, "shall be turned into hell"; by which I understand, not that he is sent off into some kind of circumvallated enclosure which is designated "Hell," but that he *himself* shall be turned into hell, that he himself shall be made it, that he himself shall become it. So that wherever he goes, on the face of the earth, or the face of the universe, hell goes; wherever he lodges, hell lodges; wherever he is, hell is. He is not merely *in* it; he *is* it! Nor does it follow either that he is it any the less because he finds for a time a certain pleasure in it. That is the reason he is it, because it is for a time a source of pleasure to him. Hell is a pleasure, of course, a certain kind of pleasure, or there would not be any hell, but it is not a kind that lasts. There is sting in the pleasure, and the sting stings; with poison in its sting, and blight, and ruin, and loss, and disease, and corruption, and death!

That is what sin is; and that is what hell is; or that is what follows sin, everywhere in the universe, because everywhere in the universe God is, prescribing everywhere that law of righteousness in it, which none of His moral creatures can sin against or break, without being turned into, and made to become, hell!

Sin, therefore, my friends, is not a thing to trifle with. It is not a thing to play with. It is not a thing to laugh with. It is not a thing to laugh at. There is nothing amusing in sin, for the end thereof is hell, is always hell. Sin is not a thing to be lightly regarded by us; for sin is hell, or becomes hell, with the sting and the poison of hell, than which there is no other sting so sharp, no other poison so deadly!

And yet, how often to-day is it lightly regarded by us. By the literature of the day, or much of it at least, whose boasted photographic realism, depicting things that are, is but another and synonymous term for a pornographic realism, depicting things that are, indeed, but things that ought not to be; things that are filthy and vile. Is it not a significant fact, that in perhaps the most popular novel of this decade, sin is represented not as heinousness, but simply as unsophisticatedness, as the more or less innocent ignorance of established social convention; and that the principal character in it, from which the book receives its name, if not immoral is unmoral, and destitute apparently for the greater part of her life of any moral sense?

By the physical science of to-day sin is lightly regarded; and is represented by it as the consequence simply of birth, or the consequence simply of environment, or the consequence perhaps of both. And people sin to-day, in New York, and elsewhere, because, born *as* they are, and also *where* they are, by forces without and within, of vicinage and heredity which they cannot control, they seem to be almost foreordained to sin; and, as far indeed as they are concerned, to sin is not sinful.

By people themselves to-day, or many of them at least, sin is lightly regarded. I do not mean by those who openly and brazenly sin and without apparently any conscience in their sinning. I mean those of a better sort, who have a conscience in regard to sin, and who never for a moment expect that they themselves will commit the sinful things which they think about at times. But they think about them, they talk about them, they read about them, in newspapers and books, they let them come into their speech, they let them come into their heart, they let them come into their mind; they think about them. And *thoughts*, deliberately entertained, as some wise person has said, are the beginnings of actions. Coming once, they come again; they strengthen, they develop, they grow. Some day they issue forth in such persons, from the invisible into the visible; and before almost they know it, they have made their bed in hell!

For, no matter how much at first men may trifle with sin, play with it, amuse themselves with it, palliate and excuse it, or lightly esteem and regard it, they find sooner or later that sin is hell, and that hell indeed is a fact!

Now, having said this much about the fact of hell, let me go on to say a little about the fate of hell.

Because God everywhere is, hell is. For the same reason precisely, because God everywhere is, there must surely come a day when it shall be said of hell that it is not. For if God everywhere is, He is where the sinner is. And no matter what the hell into which for a time he may turn himself and become, God is with him in it. And if God is with him in it, God at last, because He is God, will win and conquer in it.

Yes, hell is, the Bible says. Sin is hell. The sinner is hell. Wherever he is, hell is, says the Bible; and philosophy and experience confirm it.

But hell is, with two doors, one into and the other out of it, with both of them open and free. And those who enter by one shall exit by the other, and from it at last escape; for God is with them in it. Yes, hell is; like a furnace of fire it is, figuratively, of course; yet really. Like an everlasting furnace of fire, burning in the universe, burning always, burning those who sin, or who through sin are in it, but who indeed shall not be always in it, for God is with them in it. For everywhere is God, His voice speaking to men, His spirit pleading with men, His power working with men; immanent in them all, present with them all, His righteous law at last prevailing over all.

Everywhere is God. Nowhere is He not. In the heights, in the depths, nowhere is He not. And even though, as the Psalmist says, I make my bed in hell, behold, Thou art there!

That, as I interpret it, is the message of the Bible, or of the Christian religion to men. Hell indeed is a fact. Sin is hell; the sinner is hell. And no matter where he sins, in New York, or in some other place, or how he sins, or why, whether because of heredity, or whether because of environment—that may be the reason of the sin, but it does not change the fact; as that may be the reason of his bodily plague and disease, heredity and environment, but it does not change the fact—he sins, and sin is hell! And yet, no matter where he sins, in this world, or some other, or why and how he sins; with the power of God working in him, he may at last cease from sin, and from the hell go free. Yes, and he shall go free. The righteousness that makes his sin a hell shall deliver him from his hell. For that righteousness is love, a punishing love, a chastening love, a cleansing love, but a never-forsaking love. And love will conquer every sin and every hell destroy.

Hence, we read of Him Who was and is the expression of that everlasting righteousness of love; that He descended into hell; the deep, dark, invisible under-world, to preach the gospel of love to the spirits there confined. He descended into hell! Love always descends into hell. It can't help it. If there is a hell on earth, or anywhere else, love will go into it. Love always descends into hell; it can't help it, for the sake of those it loves. And to every person there that never-forsaking love speaks, saying, "O, turn thee, turn thee, turn thee, to thy God!" And turn at last the sinner must, and will. And that righteousness of love will in the end prevail.

That is the message of the Christian religion to us. Sin is a fact, a heinous fact. Hell is a fact, an awful fact. But it is also a fact that God is with us in it, suffering with us in it, to save and redeem us from it. It is the message of the Christian religion to men, and should also be the message of the Christian Church to men—to all men everywhere; never condoning sin, never palliating sin, but giving to the sinner an everlasting hope; causing every sinner on the face of the earth, no matter what his sin or how excuseless his sin, to say with the Psalmist,

"Though I make my bed in hell, behold, Thou art there!" And to hear there the voice, saying, "Rise, and walk!"

THE VISION OF HEAVEN.

Thy brother shall rise again.—ST. JOHN xi. 23.

THE VISION OF HEAVEN.

This is the season in the ecclesiastical year, this Easter season, when our thoughts are directed to the consideration of that great hope of immortality which has always been, in all ages, in all lands, and among all peoples, savage and civilized, barbarous and enlightened, the hope of human life. Let us consider that hope for a little while this morning, as it seems to be interpreted through the language of the text by the Christian religion to us, or by the teaching of Jesus Christ; and which, when put in topical form, may be expressed as follows: The Hope of the Perpetuation of Ourselves as Involving in it the Hope of the Perpetuation of our Relationships.

First let us inquire what it is that constitutes "ourselves"? And what is it? Our bodies? Hardly that, for our bodies are constantly changing, and crumbling and perishing and passing away, while we ourselves remain. What is it then? Our characters? That is coming a little nearer to it. And yet I think we can come a little nearer than that. For what is it that forms our characters, fashions, shapes, moulds them, makes them what they are? Our loves; the things we love to do, the pursuits we love to follow, the actions we love to perform, the people we love to love. These are the things, these loves, or these exercisings in us of love, which precipitate in us that deposit which we call in the aggregate our characters; which, in their last analysis, are resolvable into our loves.

Our loves, therefore, are our characters. Our loves are ourselves. And when we express the hope that we ourselves after death, or notwithstanding death, may still go on, somehow, and be perpetuated, we are but expressing the hope that our loves may still go on and be perpetuated.

That was the hope, or that was the desire at least, which the sister of Lazarus had. She loved her brother. She wanted to go on loving her brother. *She* could not go on without that love; for that love was part of herself; it was herself; and she herself could not go on and be herself without it. That was what the hope of immortality meant to her, as far as she had that hope. That, when we come to think about it and analyze it, is what it means to everybody else; not the hope of the perpetuation of himself without his loves, his various human loves whatever they may be, but the hope of the perpetuation of himself with his loves. For without his human loves, his various human loves, he could not be himself, he would be somebody else; and he does not want to be somebody else; he wants to be himself. That is why the heathen pupil of the Christian missionary, of whom we have all heard, did not want to go to the missionary's heaven. When the missionary told him, speaking I think more zealously than truthfully, that none of his ancestors would be there because they had not been baptized: "Will my father not be there, he asked nor my mother; my brother, my kinsfolk, my ancestors?" Then he did not want to go there; he wanted to go where they were; for he loved them and wanted to go on loving them. *He* could not go on without that love, for that love was part of himself, was himself, and he himself could not go on and be himself without it.

Neither can we. Without that love within us, that human love within us, that love which makes our characters, that love which makes ourselves, that love which is ourselves; we cannot go on without it, for it is we! If we are to go on and live, *it* must go on, that human love within us. *It* must go on and live, or we cannot go on.

This far then we have come in the development of our subject, and this much we have seen—that we ourselves cannot be perpetuated without the perpetuation in us of that human love, or of those human loves which are ourselves, and without the perpetuation of which we ourselves as ourselves cannot be perpetuated.

Now let us advance a little further in the development of the subject. How can those human loves be perpetuated without the perpetuation of those relationships in which those loves exist? For love is a relative term. We cannot love nothing; love is a relative term and implies something to love; as seeing is a relative term, and hearing is a relative term. Unless there be something to see we cannot see; unless there be something to hear we cannot hear; unless there be something to love we cannot love. And if that love is to go on, that something which it loves must go on, or that relation in which it is exercised must go on. Otherwise *it* cannot go on, it cannot be exercised, and the love cannot exist. And if the love cannot exist, the great, complex, manifold love that makes us what we are, how can we exist? How can we think of ourselves as existing? We cannot. And that is why we find it so hard sometimes to think of ourselves as existing in another world, because we try to think of ourselves existing there, in that other world, out of all relation to what we love in this world, and to whom we love in this world. And we cannot do it; it is impossible. But according to Jesus Christ that is not the case. And that hope of immortality, which nothing can eradicate from the human heart, does not mean and involve the perpetuation of ourselves, or the perpetuation of the loves which are ourselves, apart from those relationships in which they now exist; it is the hope of the perpetuation of those relationships. *Thy* brother shall rise again—not simply the man Lazarus whose body lies in yonder grave—but then as now, there as here, *thy* brother! They are to be perpetuated; those relationships, in which here and now we exercise our love; they are to be perpetuated, in that other life, in that other world. There as here the same, making us the same, or keeping us the same; loving there what here we love, and in those same relations in which we love here; which though broken now for a time, are healed again and restored!

That is the great human hope of some immortal life, as it seems to be through the medium of the text, through the language of Jesus Christ, interpreted to us; the hope of the perpetuation, not merely of our present selves or of our present loves, but of those various relationships in which our present loves are exercised.

I know of course that there are difficulties connected with this view. Perhaps there are some embarrassments. For some of the relationships in which our loves at present are exercised may not be pure and good; but sensuous, and corrupt; and we cannot possibly think that they will still go on; for corruption cannot inherit incorruption. But there are other relationships of love which are pure and good, noble and ennobling, which we can easily think of as going on; and which, according to Jesus Christ, as I interpret His teaching, shall go on and be perpetuated.

May I mention two or three of them in the way of illustration? The relationship of Home; that domestic relationship, so sacred, so divine, where our human love begins, where first we learn to love, and find the meaning of love; that garden soil of Home which no rude hand must touch, no trespasser destroy, no violater invade; where love in all its sweetness, in all its beauty, grows; which seems to be, and is, on earth like the paradise of God; but which is broken by death at times and blasted and destroyed. No, says Jesus Christ; it is not destroyed. That Home, or that home relationship does still exist, and shall forever exist. Thy brother shall rise again! And the home which ministered here to love, making us what we are, shall minister there to love, keeping us what we are!

The relationship of Home; the relationship of Country. For we are not only placed in homes, we are placed in lands, or nations. The relationship of Country, ministering to what we call the "patriotic" love; a love so strong and high, so deep and great within us, that it sometimes consumes the love of Home within us; which, as we feel its joy within us, thrilling us, inspiring us, casting out for a time at least the love of self within us, seems to be almost like the love of God within us!

Shall it not go on? Shall we find no country there, in that other life, in that other world, to stir and kindle in us there the patriotic love; no national shrine or altar there, to inspire it there within us, to keep it there alive? Yes; it seems to me Jesus Christ declares, that national bond of brotherhood which does here exist, in some exalted shape and form shall continue there to exist. Thy brother—O, thou patriot heart—whom here thou dost serve, whom here thou dost love; thy brother shall rise again, where all the peoples, and tribes, and kindreds, and tongues, and nations of the earth are gathered! And the patriotic love which thou here hast felt, making thee what thou art, thou shalt continue to feel, keeping thee what thou art!

The relationship of Home, the relationship of Country, and then that great and wide and widening relationship of Humanity, which ministers to what we call the "philanthropic" love, which to-day we are coming so strongly in our hearts to feel; going beyond the home, going beyond the nation, which by man in coming years will more and more be felt, disposing him to serve on earth and help his brother man. It too shall go on. It too shall be perpetuated, the philanthropic love—Thy brother shall rise again; a real humanity there, to serve, to help, to love, to minister unto, as a real humanity here!

Home, Country, Humanity. These are some of the great cardinal relationships—there are others—in which now we live, in which now we grow, becoming now what we are, becoming now ourselves; nor can we in some other world, some future world, some heavenly world, be ourselves without them. According to Jesus Christ we shall not be without them. Home, Country, Humanity; great, cardinal relationships ministering here to love, and making us what we are; in higher, purer, better, more enduring form shall minister there to love, keeping us what we are.

So does Jesus Christ interpret that great human hope of immortality, which has always been and always will be the hope of human life, making it more attractive, more appealing to us, more human to us; whose voice it seems to me we can hear to-day, standing by the grave of our broken hopes and loves, and saying to every man: "Thy brother, whom thou seest, whom thou knowest, whom thou lovest now, in the Home-world, in the Nation-world, in the great Human-world, thou shalt hereafter see, thou shalt hereafter know, thou shalt hereafter love; for thy brother shall rise again!"

THE VISION OF GOOD MAKING EVIL.

Is thine eye evil, because I am good?—St. Matthew xx. 15

THE VISION OF GOOD MAKING EVIL.

THAT is from the parable of the laborers in the vineyard which you have just heard read as the Gospel for the day. It is quite likely that some of you on hearing it read thought that there was in fact some injustice in it, and that those who had worked for a day were in fairness entitled to more than those who had worked for an hour, when they had all been doing apparently the same kind of work. That, perhaps, is what some of you thought. That is what some of the laborers thought, and to which they gave expression, in murmuring and complaining. And why? Because the vineyard owner had not been good to them? No; but because, while good to them, he had been good to others. That suggests the subject on which I wish to speak—Looking at ourselves with reference to others; or Good making evil. Or still again, The Paradox of Goodness.

First, see how it was in the parable itself. Here were certain persons sent into a certain vineyard by the vineyard owner, to do a certain kind of work,—a day's work, at a certain price, which they considered fair and equitable, if not generous, or which at all events they had agreed to take. Now, suppose no other laborers had been sent into that vineyard, at the third, the ninth, or the eleventh hour, and that they themselves, by themselves, had labored there all day, alone, with no other laborers in the vineyard. Would they then have murmured, when the time of reckoning came, because they then received what it was said they would receive and what they had agreed to receive? Would they then have murmured and complained? I think not. With the work of the day no easier, and the burden of the day no lighter, and the heat of the day no less, and the wage of the day no more, it would have been all right, honorable, equitable, fair, with nothing to complain of. Why, then, did they complain? What was it that put the evil into their eye? Because their eye, instead of looking at the vineyard owner who had sent them into the vineyard, who, when they were idle and had nothing to do, had given them something to do, and for the doing of which had promised to give them a certain sum, a certain price, and which he did give; with everything all right, honorable, fair, and nothing to complain of,—because I say their eye, instead of looking at the vineyard owner who had been so good to them, was looking over there at those other laborers in it, to whom the vineyard owner had also been so good. That is what did it; that is what put the evil into their eye, trickling down into the heart and spreading there its slime; making it evil!

That is what did it in their case; that is what does it in ours. Looking at ourselves not with reference to God, the great vineyard Owner, and what He has done for us, but looking at ourselves with reference to others and what He has done for them—that is the way in which the evil that is in us is created in us, our eye evil, because God is so good! God does not make evil, for God is good, supremely good, with nothing but goodness in Him, nothing but goodness emanating from Him. God does not create evil; He could not! And yet, paradoxical as the statement seems, or is, it is the goodness of God that *does* create it at times! Just as the coming together of two gases will sometimes make a third gas that is different from either; so does the goodness of God, and the giving of good things to others, God and they together, He giving good things, and they receiving good things, make in us at times things that are not good.

In some such way as that, I suppose, the devil

might have been made. God did not make the devil. God is good, with nothing but goodness—that is necessary to the conception of a God—emanating from Him. God did not make the devil; He could not! And yet it was the goodness of God perhaps that did make him. Originally he was—so at least the Scriptures seem to teach and imply, and all religious fancyings and imaginings about him—originally he was, not an angel of darkness but an angel of light, to whom God was good. But in the spiritual hierarchy of that supramundane sphere there were other angels of light—so again the Scriptures seem to teach and imply—to whom God was also good, very good; and who were perhaps in the goodness of God faring better than he. And looking at and seeing, that goodness of God to them, the evil entered into his eye, into his heart, lodging and dwelling there, making him evil, making him a devil. So, I say, the devil might have been created in the other world. Whether or not he was so created is of course a matter of conjecture; but it is not a matter of conjecture, but of experience and observation so far as this world is concerned. And whatever the way in which the devil there was made, that is the way in which the devil here is made, that is the way in which the devils here are made, for there are many of them, their name is legion; and goodness makes them! That is the paradox of goodness, that it makes devils!

Is that strange? Yes, it is strange; but it is true. Did not the goodness of Jesus Christ make devils? Not Jesus Christ Himself, no, not Jesus Christ Himself, in His aim, His motive, His purpose, which was nothing but love, compassion, benevolence, but the goodness of Jesus Christ; did not it make devils all about Him; and as He persisted uncompromisingly in His goodness to the end, did it not make more devils about Him, until at last they killed Him? Would it be so now? I do not know. It might be. What I do know is this, that looking at a goodness in others which is better than the goodness in us, and therefore rebuking and putting to shame the goodness in us; creates at times in us, antagonisms to it. We do not want such goodness. We do not want it about us. It is too good. And we shun and avoid and dislike it, and sometimes despise and hate it, and would not be sorry perhaps if some one else should kill it or put it out of the way.

So it is with things that are morally good. So it is with things that are physically good; creating things at times that are not good, creating evil things.

What is it that is creating so many of the evil things in society to-day? The good things in it! without which the evil things would not exist; the physical wealths and treasures, the physical blessings and prosperities, which those persons have whom we call rich, those other laborers in the vineyard who do not labor much, and yet who have just as much or more perhaps than some of the rest of us who are called poor, who labor all day long, bearing all day long the burden and heat of the day. We do not like it, and we do not like them, and we murmur and complain and threaten, and are envious and angry and jealous, and are going to do something about it, we don't know what, but we are going to do something to change it. What is it that makes all this mumuring and complaining and threatening, putting all this evil into the eye, into the mind, into the heart of society to-day, making evil passions in it, making evil things? The good things in it! of which some persons seem to have so much and others not so much; and who are looking at themselves with reference to those others.

But I am not speaking to a congregation of poor

people this morning; and therefore I want to say that not only among the poor and the poorer, is this devil-making process going on, but among the rich and the richer it is also going on; prides, vanities, arrogancies, extravagancies, superficial ostentations, overstraining emulations, pageants, pomps, parades, taxing so much their time, their strength, their physical resources, that they have but little left of time or strength or physical resources for a better kind of doing and giving. Devils there are made, evils there are made, and in the same manner made. Looking at themselves with reference to others, trying to keep up with them, trying to get ahead of them, not wishing to be outdone by the good things of others, not wishing to be outshone by the good things of others; and if they have to be, then there is carping, and criticizing, and heartburning, and backbiting and murmuring and complaining: the devils come.

So again we see in society to-day, as in the old parable long ago, the good things making evil things. It is the paradox of goodness. It is, it has been, it will be, until we learn to look at ourselves, in this great vineyard-world, not with reference chiefly to others, for then the envies and the prides and the ostentations and the covetousnesses and the uncharitablenesses, and all the devils will come; but until we learn to look at ourselves, each of us, with reference chiefly to God. Laboring here, living here, with reference chiefly to God. Developing here our powers, faculties, gifts, endowments, whatever they may be, with reference chiefly to God. Fulfilling here and rounding out ourselves with reference chiefly to God, and that great ideal life of God in Jesus Christ appearing. Then, and only then, can the devils be cast out, out of ourselves and out of the world!

Without God, my friends, we cannot work this world. It has been tried and it has failed. It sometimes seems to me as though, not avowedly but virtually, we were trying it again, and again, if so, it will fail. Statesmen, politicians, financiers, men of affairs, whoever we are, even from the most practical and worldly point of view, we cannot work this world without God! And the good things that are in it, as more and more they come, looking at ourselves not with reference to God but with reference to others, will more and more make evil in it. But looking at ourselves with reference to God, the eye lifted up to Him, the point of vision is changed, the angle of vision is changed; the paradox of goodness becomes the parallax. What seemed before to be evil seems now to be good, and God seems to be good, good to us, good to others, good to all, making us and others, making all good; and more and more does this world seem to be, like all the worlds, the expression not merely of the Infinite Power or of the Infinite Wisdom, but of the Infinite goodness of God!

VISIONS IN HIGH PLACES.

And the servants of the king of Syria said unto him, Their gods are gods of the hills; therefore they were stronger than we; but let us fight against them in the plain, and surely we shall be stronger than they.—1 KINGS xx. 23.

VISIONS IN HIGH PLACES.

The armies of the king of Syria had been defeated in battle by the armies of the king of Israel, and in trying to explain the defeat, and to ascertain the cause of it, the counsellors of the Syrian king found it in the fact to which the text refers. They had been fighting the children of Israel, they said, in the wrong place, on the hills, where their gods were; and where, in consequence, the children of Israel had been especially protected and made strong; and if they could only fight them again, not on the hills but on the plains, where their gods were not, they might hope for a different result.

That was their explanation of their defeat, by their enemies. Is it the explanation of our defeat, by our enemies? Let us inquire, and see if what was said of the children of Israel, so long ago, can, with any truth, be said to-day of us, and that our gods, like their gods, are the gods of the hills.

First, let us inquire why, or in what sense, it came to be said of them.

It seems to have been the custom, in those ancient times, for the people to associate religion with high places. That is where they built their altars and their shrines, their sanctuaries and their temples; and for the very obvious reason, as has been suggested, that those high places were supposed to be a little nearer to heaven, nearer to their God, or nearer to their gods; and where, in some especial and exceptional sense, their gods were thought to dwell. When, therefore, the people of those times wanted to meet their gods, and to worship and pray and sacrifice and burn incense to their gods, that is what they had to do—they had to go up to the high places, where their gods were, where their gods lived; as in the other places, the fields, the valleys, the plains, where for the most part the people themselves were, and the people themselves lived, the gods of the people were *not*, and did not live.

That was the way in which, and the only way in which, they could become religious. So at least they thought. And that, apparently, in spite of all their teaching to the contrary, is what the children of Israel thought. This is what in fact we find throughout their whole history they were always doing—going up to the high places, building there their altars, offering there their sacrifices, thinking that there they were able to come a little nearer to God. That was not the case, so their teachers taught them, Moses and the prophets; that was not the case; they were not any nearer to God in the high places than in other places. Persistently, repeatedly, over and over they taught it; but they could not make the people see and understand it. They continued still to go to the high places, building there their altars, burning there their incense, on the high places, and giving thus the impression— and naturally enough—to their polytheistic neighbors, that the gods of the children of Israel were the gods of the hills!

And that is why they said they had been defeated by them—they had been fighting them on the hills, where their gods were. If they could only fight them again, on the plains, where their gods were not, they would experience a different result.

Well, so it was with them, and their religion; not their theoretical, but their practical religion, or their popular religion. How is it with us, and our popular religion? Are we any better and wiser? Are we not disposed, as the children of Israel were, to localize God, in the high places of the earth; not literally in the high places, but figuratively in the high places, the places we call religious, and therefore near to God, and where indeed we meet Him; as the other places are not called religious, and therefore not near to God, and where we do not meet Him, but where we do meet our enemies, the lust of the flesh, the lust of the eye, the pride of life, and where we are so often whipped and routed by them, and driven from the field?

This, for instance, is one of our high places, this House, this Church. And coming here for a little while, and dwelling here for a little while, an hour or two a week, we are dwelling near to God, in some sense, so I presume we think, and doing something religious. So in truth we are dwelling near to God, and doing something religious. How will it be to-morrow, to-morrow morning, to-morrow evening, when we are not dwelling here, but dwelling somewhere else? Will we still continue to think that we are dwelling near to God, and doing something religious; when we are traveling and trading, and bargaining and calling and shopping, and visiting, and dancing—will we still continue to think that we are dwelling near to God, just as much as now, and doing something religious just as much as now? We ought to think it, for it is true. So our Christian teachers and our Christian creeds declare. But will we think it true; will we feel it true? Or will we find it hard as the children of Israel did to think and feel it true?

We will find it hard, very hard, to feel that there we are dwelling as near to God as here. And all our old temptations, our old besetting sins, our vanities, our prides, our passions, seem indeed to know that we will find it hard. Therefore they do not fight us here, or they do not fight us here so much; or if they do, we rise above them here, we overcome them here; for here we seem to be dwelling near to God, as in His presence, with His atmosphere about us, feeling here a little His protecting help, receiving here a little His quickening strength. But just wait, they seem to say, these enemies of ours, these vanities, these prides, these passions, these grasping and covetous ambitions—just wait till we get these religious people down there, on the plains; in the clubrooms, in the ballrooms, in the banqueting-rooms, in all their social places, their market places and their other places; just wait till we get these religious people down on the plains—not on the hills where their gods are, but on the plains where they are not, and then you will see that we shall be stronger than they, and that we shall overcome them there.

And so they often do. And for the reason that

our gods are not the gods of the valleys, and the plains, but like the children of Israel's gods, they are only the gods of the hills.

Let me try to make it clearer, with another illustration.

Are we not disposed, when we think of God, to think of Him as up there, somewhere, we do not know where exactly, but away up there, somewhere, at some great distance from us, on some distant throne perhaps, in some distant heaven, where the angels are, and the archangels, and the cherubim, and the seraphim, and all the heavenly hosts, and where He rules and governs and has so much to do with all that is going on? And if, while living here, we would try to seek His kingdom, we must try to seek it there, in heaven, among the angels; putting ourselves in sympathy with what is going on there, in heaven, and not so much in sympathy with what is going on here, upon the earth, and among the people here. We must be separate and apart a little from what is going on among the people here, the interests here of the people, the struggles here of the people, the betterments here of the people, their social betterments, their political betterments, their recreational or their educational betterments, their betterments here on the earth. These things we say are temporal, and worldly. We, as religious persons, if we want to be very religious, must not minister unto these things. We must go apart from these things and minister unto other things: and, instead of putting ourselves in sympathy with the people here, on the earth, and what they are trying to do, we must put ourselves in sympathy with the angels, there, in heaven, and what *they* are trying to do.

And the consequence is, my friends, so far as that is the case, that these great absorbing interests, these secular and earthly interests, are going on so much without religion to-day. And the people absorbed in them, and who have to be absorbed in them, are going on so much without religion to-day! For that is a kind of religion, a religion of the heavenly hills, or of the heavenly hilltops, that the people cannot reach to day, and do not need to-day, and do not want to-day! And they are right; they ought not to want it! And if we are to make and keep this religion of ours strong upon the earth, an appealing power on earth, redeeming and conquering the earth, we must somehow try to make it live and move and be upon the earth, in the midst of the interests, in the midst of the struggles, of the people on the earth.

That ought to be our way, but that is not our way.

> "The parish priest of Austerity
> Climbed up in a high Church steeple
> To be nearer God; so that he might hand
> His word down to his people.
> And in sermon script he daily wrote
> What he thought was sent from heaven;
> And he dropped this down on his people's heads
> Two times one day in seven.
> In his age, God said, 'Come down and die!'
> And he cried from out the steeple —
> 'Where art Thou, Lord?' And the Lord replied,
> 'Down here, among my people!'"

Ah, yes, so He is, and so we must learn to find Him, down here, on the earth, revealing here His presence, and through, and by means of, and in the midst of all our kingdoms, establishing here His kingdom; giving here a heaven, not merely when we die, but here on the earth a heaven; or giving to us here, not merely when we die, but here upon the earth, something like the joy and the peace and the gladdening inspiration of a heavenly music to us!

That is religion. Not something that we go and touch every now and then, up in the high places, and then run away from, until the time comes to go back and touch it again, in the high places. That religion is passing away. It is almost gone.

It will not do to-day. For religion is something within us, always within us, in all places. Religion is a life—if you please to call it so, it is a culture, God's culture; or, better still it is a faith, which looks out upon the world, as the great and wonderful Sacrament of the Almighty God, with its outward and visible sign and its inward and spiritual grace.

A life, a culture, a faith. Like the poet's faith, to whom in all the physical light that lightens land and sea, another light appears. The artist's faith, who, in all the varied forms of the physical beauty about him, another beauty sees. The musician's faith, who, as the surging waves of sound strike upon his ear, another wave of sound is made to hear and feel, deeper, sweeter, mightier, surging through his soul. The prophet's faith, who, in all the happenings of things upon the earth, some great enduring truth and enduring principle sees. The philosopher's faith, who, with his philosophic and penetrating insight, sees the spiritual in the physical, the eternal in the temporal, the ideal in the real. And the poet's faith, and the artist's, the musician's, the prophet's, the philosopher's, suggesting some one greater faith as comprehending all, gathering all their fugitive and fragmentary forms in some integrating wholeness—that is the Christian's faith, seeing in the world, and in all the world, the presence of God revealed! He goes up from time to time, to his high places, to commune there with his God, not because He is nowhere else, and can nowhere else be found; but, lifting up his eyes to the hills, whence cometh his strength, to find Him everywhere; in the fields, the valleys, the plains, where his life is, where his enemies are, his temptations, his trials, his wearinesses, his despondencies, his besetting sins; to meet them there, and defeat them there, as in the presence there of God!

That is religion. How great it is! How good it is! A faith, a culture, a life, shining more and more in its ever-brightening path, as unto some perfect day; breaking, like the morning dawn, over the heavenly hills of God, as the sunshine after the rain!

VISIONS IN THE WILDERNESS.

Then was Jesus led up of the Spirit into the wilderness to be tempted of the devil.—ST. MATTHEW iv. 1.

VISIONS IN THE WILDERNESS.

It is characteristic, I believe, of the names of the Alpine Mountains, or many of them at least, that they are derived from the peculiar shape, or size, or color, or other physical aspect of the mountains themselves. One of them, however, has derived its name not from its own individuality and configuration, but from the vast extent of the varied and tangled vegetable growth that clusters around its base, and is known among its fellows in that marvelous range, in distinction from all the others, as the Mountain of the Meadows, or more familiarly "The Matterhorn."

The season of Lent through which we are passing gives us the thought of God, not as clothed with those attributes of strength and glory and unapproachable splendor peculiar to Himself, sitting high and lifted up upon His exalted throne as the great and wonderful God of creation, but as the God of the wilderness, campaigning here on earth amid our hardships here, sharing our infirmities, enduring our privations, engaging in our conflicts with the world, the flesh and the devil; having more or less of our varied, tangled, tempted human life about Him; as the God of the Wilderness.

And it is of that God of the Wilderness, or more familiarly "The Temptation of Jesus Christ" that I wish this morning to speak.

It is not an easy subject to preach upon, for it is not easy to understand how, if Jesus Christ was God as well as man He could be tempted at all. When, therefore, we read that He was tempted in all points like as we are, it is hard to avoid thinking or feeling that those temptations were not real and actual like those which we encounter, but that they correspond to ours simply in appearance, phantom forms upon His part of most substantial and painful experiences upon ours. By virtue of His being God He was the possessor of infinite and inexhaustible resources; and how could such a one feel as we do the pressure of human limitations and weaknesses, or experience as we do the stress of human needs and passions?

It is easy to state the difficulty and to state it strongly. It is not so easy to answer it. I shall not try where so many others have failed, except to say this: that it is not a difficulty which appertains exclusively to the thought of Jesus Christ as God, but appertains as well to any thought of God. For if God is to be apprehended by us with any definiteness or clearness of apprehension He must be apprehended by us through the medium of man, through the image and the likeness of man. God is spirit. Yes; but what is spirit? Can we think it, by itself, apart from all portrayal and attempted expression of it? We can use the word "spirit," but it will have no meaning for us until in our thought at least we give it human shape, likeness, image, substance. The ghost must be bodied forth, not physically perhaps, but mentally, in some kind of mental picture, otherwise the word "ghost" will have no meaning for us. So with the word "God." Unless in our minds we can body it forth in some kind of human likeness, some kind of human picture, having human features, and properties and parts, and passions; the word "God" will have no meaning for us.

Is not that in fact precisely what we do when we try to think of God, to body Him forth a little in some kind of human embodiment, giving a human name, a human intelligence to Him, human pity, and love, and personality to Him, using those words as we have learned to use them in our human speech? Try to think of God in any other way with nothing human about Him, having no human endowments, or properties, or affections, with nothing human about Him, and you will find you cannot do it. Just as soon as you begin to think of God with any kind of clearness you begin to think of Him with some kind of humanness. If, then, it be true, that God in order to be apprehended by us at all, must be apprehended by us through some kind of human picturing; it also follows as true, that in that human picturing of Him, we bring Him within the range of human limitations, needs, wants, experiences. So that the difficulty of understanding how, if Jesus Christ was God He could be tempted, does not appertain exclusively to the thought of Jesus Christ as God, but to any thought of God apart from Jesus Christ. Such a thought is of necessity a human thought, a thought that makes Him more or less human to us. We cannot think of God in any other way. In Himself He may be some other way; but that at least is the way in which He is to us, in which now at least He is apprehended by us, as having more or less of our human life, our tried and tempted human life clustered and gathered about Him.

That, too, is the way in which, now at least, we need to apprehend Him; not so much as the great God sitting upon His throne and calling to the stars in the order of their course, but as God in the wilderness, Who knows and understands and feels our tempted life: *a tempted God!* If you tell me that God *cannot* be tempted, I answer possibly not. I know nothing about the divine nature in the abstract. Apart from all human parallels and likenesses I cannot conceive of Him. I know nothing about the nature of God in the abstract, but what I do know is this: *I* can be tempted; I *am* tempted; and as a tempted man I must somehow find a God Who knows what temptation is. My life is out in the wilderness, doing battle there, with the evil forces there, with the evil voices there; day by day I meet them; day by day I feel them; the pain of the poise so sharp at times between the good and the bad, the expedient and the right. Every day some duty comes in an unattractive form, and with it the impulse to run away or avoid it. The lust of the flesh is mine; and the lust of the eye is mine; and the pride of life is mine. My life is out in the wilderness fighting with the devil; and I must somehow find a God Who is fighting the devil with me, and helping me to fight him!

That is the kind of God Whom now we need. That is the kind of God Whom in Jesus Christ we find. God in the Wilderness where we are, fighting the devil.

Will you come with me a few minutes into that wilderness to see what kind of a wilderness it is? I think we shall find that it is the same kind of a wilderness, substantially, in which we are; and that the same kind of fighting is going on in it.

"Then was Jesus led up of the Spirit into the wilderness to be tempted of the devil." Then: When? When, in connection with His baptism which had just taken place, there was awakened in Him the consciousness of His great and wonderful power. Then, the temptation came. Then, it always comes. We speak of the weak as tempted. So they are. But the strong are also tempted; in some respects I think they are tempted more than the weak. It is not the little average-man, with no ambition in him and no fire of passion in him, who is tempted the most to go wrong. It is the man above the average, with a great ambition in him, with a great fierce force of slumbering passion in him; with exceptional gifts and powers, and with exceptional opportunities in which to display those gifts with some improper display, in which to use those powers with some improper use; he is the man who is tempted most to go wrong. The man who has great talent, and knows and feels that he has it, other things being equal, is tempted more than the man who has but little talent. And the woman who has great beauty, other things being equal, is tempted more than the woman who has but little beauty. The consciousness of any kind of gift, physical gift, mental gift, the gift of money endowment, brings always I think great temptations with it. The man who has within him a power which lifts him up above his fellow men will see more things to do, not only good but bad, not only right but wrong, than they can possibly see; and will be tempted to do them. He may not yield to the temptation, but he sees it, and will flush and burn with it at times. The consciousness of his power, of his gift, will have the effect to drive him into the wilderness of integrity and virtue, and purity, struggling with the evil voices!

When, therefore, there came in some mysterious way, which I cannot explain, to Jesus Christ in connection with His baptism, the consciousness of His great, unique and marvelous power, *then*, "straightway," "immediately," He was led up of the Spirit, into the wilderness to be tempted of the devil. For forty days the conflict lasts; then the reaction comes. In the three great temptations which there He meets and faces, we seem to see all the varied issues of that prolonged and secret encounter brought out into the foreground and culminated.

He is represented first as being tempted by the suggestion to use and employ for Himself—a very natural suggestion under the circumstances, in his weak and exhausted condition—to use and employ for Himself the powers bestowed upon Him for the Kingdom of God; to make bread out of the stones about Him. It will be a misuse of the power, He might have thought or said, and therefore not right; but it is necessary to live, and that will make it right! The surrounding circumstances of the temptation were peculiar to Jesus Christ : the temptation itself comes to us all. The preacher, the lawyer, the banker, the professional man as well as the man in business, are all in many and various ways tempted to make bread out of stone, to perpetrate fraud, and wrong, injury, and crime; not because these things are desirable in themselves or because they want to do them, but because as they also say, it is necessary to live. Truth has been bartered, and sacrificed; virtue has been defiled; purity has been sullied; honor has been trailed in the dust, because *it is necessary to live!* And the lips have sworn to a lie; and the hands have been stretched out to do what the conscience behind condemns, *because it is necessary to live!* The merchant has yielded to what he knows is wrong, *because it is necessary to live;* and the clergyman has conformed to what he knows is false; and the woman has succumbed to what she knows is shame, *because it is necessary to live!*

It is the subtlest of all the subtle temptations met and encountered by us; and half the sins and shames of New York City are engendered by it. And Jesus Christ met it, met it and overcame it, going down beneath it to the deeper truth, and showing that not by bread alone, but by every word that proceedeth out of the mouth of God is it necessary to live. And if I must think of God in some kind of human form and image, I will think of Him as a God, Who, having been tempted as I am to make bread out of stone; can help me to conquer as He also conquered.

Then the devil taketh Him into the Holy City and setteth Him upon a pinnacle of the Temple, and said: "If thou be the Son of God cast thyself down!" How all this was done I do not know; but it is a marvelous picture. No classic writer of Greece or Rome has ever portrayed such a picture as that. And the artist who painted it, must surely have been inspired to be able thus to show by a stroke, by a single stroke, what the sin of presumption is; how human it is; how natural it is; how we are all tempted by it! Try your powers on. Put them to the test. Cast yourself down, and let it be seen that what has harmed others cannot hurt you. All the way through life we are tempted by it. The young man is tempted by it. Conscious then of his strength, or what he calls his strength; heedless then of advice, so often in fact despising it; unwilling to be warned; thinking that he knows better than any one else what he is about; he runs into risks and dangers, he exposes himself to perils, he casts himself down for a time, it is only to be for a time, into careless and reckless living, presuming upon the strengths and immunities, upon the angels of his youthfulness to bear him up, lest he should dash his foot against a stone! And the old man is tempted by it. He is wiser now, and sadder, through the lessons taught by experience, and yet still feels quite equal to all the evils about him, and the difficulties that beset him. Master of himself and his destiny, and holding the reins in his own right hand; there is time enough yet to think about God and religion; time enough yet to think about that of which the minister speaks so much, a public confession of Jesus Christ in His Church; time enough yet to think about that! And the years go quickly by; and suddenly some day they come to an end, and he casts himself down—he has to now—from the pinnacle of the temple of life into the valley of the shadow of death, presuming upon the mercy of God, and hoping that His angels will somehow bear him up, and keep him from being hurt, as he plunges into that dark and unknown depth!

Ah, yes, all the way through life, in all the stations of life we are tempted by it; to cast ourselves down, to do the thing that is not quite right; tampering with the moneys given to us in trust; jeopardizing the talents given to us in trust; imperiling the lives given to us in trust; hazarding the souls given to us in trust, presuming upon some special protection or immunity that will be vouchsafed to us, to keep us from being hurt by that which has so often, and so fatally, so many others hurt.

Then the devil taketh Him up into an exceeding high mountain and showeth Him all the kingdoms of the world, and the glory of them—what a sight it must have been!—and saith, "All these things will I give Thee if Thou wilt worship me!" Was it a real mountain? Was it a real devil? Was it a real world whose glory he showed Him? Again I say I do not know. But it is a marvelous picture, vividly, strikingly portrayed; and the temptation which it depicts,—who of us has not felt it? Who of us has not yielded to it at times, and tried to win some glory, some success in life by worshipping the devil and doing homage to Satan? Who of us at times, for the sake of some worldly end, some worldly honor, some worldly popularity and gratification has not taken counsel, not with the highest and best in him but with the basest and worst, not with the voice of God in him but with the voice of the devil? The glory of the world: how bright, how beautiful, how alluring it is! How it fascinates the heart! We would all like if we could to subdue the world and make its treasures ours. We would all like if we could to win the world and make its honors ours. Jesus Christ had the power to do it. Jesus Christ, I believe, was tempted to do it, in a way that seemed to Him wrong; in a way that did not seem to be the way of God. "Go, with thy great, marvelous power; build thy kingdom up; gird thee with thy sword upon thy thigh; ride on in thy majesty and thy right hand shall teach thee terrible things!" Capable of building up His kingdom on the earth by sheer force and power, He will build it up in truth and love; and at whatsoever cost by being true Himself.

"Get thee behind me, Satan, thou adversary of God!" Then the angels came and ministered unto Him; love, joy, peace, patience, faith, hope; and have ministered ever since unto the hearts in which He dwells.

The God of the Wilderness, with our tangled, tried, and tempted human life gathered and clustered around Him: Most wonderful picture of God; most human picture of God; most helpful picture of God! That is the picture of God we need, fighting our battles here in the wilderness; of a God Who knows what the wilderness is and will help us to fight. And when in the wilderness we faint, and fall, and yield to temptation in it, the God of the wilderness knows how hard is the fight, and will pity and pardon and lift us up again.

Wonderful picture of God! Helpful picture of God! May it help us in the wilderness to fight our wilderness fight; and, like Jesus Christ, at last to win our victories in it!

THE VISION OF SOCIAL UNITY.

Having made known unto us the mystery of his will: That in the dispensation of the fulness of times he might gather together in one all things in Christ, both which are in heaven, and which are on earth; even in him.—EPHESIANS i. 9, 10.

THE VISION OF SOCIAL UNITY.

That is a magnificent dream. Is it anything more? Will it ever be realized? Will it ever come to pass? Will the time ever come when the ascendency in this world of Jesus Christ shall be universal and complete? Christian people believe that it will, and from that faith derive the courage for their work. But when will it come? And how? What are the signs of its coming? Are there any signs just now of its coming? If there are, what are they? Let me try to answer these questions, and show you how I think this world will at last become a Christian world, not merely in name but in fact, and all things in it be gathered up into Jesus Christ.

First, let me try to show you how the human mind to-day, apart from religion, seems to be working in that direction. If you have observed with any closeness the trend of modern thought, you will of course have noticed that it is a tendency toward unity of conception; that it has been characterized, in other words, by the effort to discover some uniting bond or principle in things, and thus to bring it possible oneness out of diversity. It is through the exercising of that tendency that many of those phenomena in the material world, which seemed at first to have no mutual connection, have been resolved at last into some common source, and have been shown to be united by some common law. That is what has given—that tendency of the modern mind to resolve the many into the one— that is what has given the physical sciences to us; Astronomy, Botany, Geology, and all the physical sciences. That is the way in which those sciences have come. In spite of the great number of the heavenly bodies, and of the great and vast distances, almost immeasurable between them, there is something nevertheless, so it has been found, which they have in common; and the science of Astronomy has come. In spite of the great number of terrestrial plants, and the great variety, almost infinite, among them, there is something nevertheless, so it has been found, which they have in common; and the science of Botany has come.

So throughout all the different spheres and departments of the physical world, the human mind has been steadily and slowly moving on toward unity of conception, has been characterized more and more by the tendency to bring together many things and divers things into one. Nor has it been contented to stop even there, but has gone on further to find, or to try at least to find, not only how all the heavenly bodies are related to one another, not only how all the plants and trees are related to one another, and all the rocks, and all the animals are related to one another, but how all the phenomena of the universe itself are related to one another, and all the kingdoms in it are related to one another; the mineral kingdom to the vegetable kingdom, the vegetable kingdom to the animal kingdom, the animal kingdom to the human kingdom—how all the phenomena of the universe itself, including even man, are related to one another.

That is what the theory of Evolution means. That is why that theory is such an appealing theory to the minds of men to-day; not because it has been verified and proved, and beyond all question established; for it has not been. But simply because it gives such satisfaction to that strong innate tendency of the human mind to-day to bring together many things, all things, and to gather them up into one.

Now, that same tendency to find, or to try at least to find, some principle of unity in the midst of a vast diversity, has been asserting itself of late, not only in connection with the phenomena of the material world, but in connection with the phenomena of the social world as well; in connection with human life. Hence we see to-day that people are trying to ascertain by patient search and study, not only the true history of the past, but the true philosophy of the history of the past, the true principle of philosophic unity running through the history of the past. They are trying not only to ascertain what is the true history of Greece and Rome and Egypt and Germany and the Anglo-Saxon world, but how to bring all those histories together, to gather them up into one, to make their history one, connected and united, one form, one life, one growth, one social life and growth. And here it is that we meet the Evolutionist again, who tells us that the unifying principle in the material world is the same unifying principle which we see in the social world; that the social world has been evolved just like the physical world; that it has been from the beginning marked by a struggle for existence, in which the weakest members have perished and succumbed, and only the strongest have survived.

What that means when translated into plain

English is Selfishness. By Selfishness, it is said, the social world to-day has come to be what it is, everybody trying to do the most he can for himself, and considering others only when he finds that that is for himself the prudent course to take.

Now, however right and good that principle of Selfishness may be when applied to the animal world and all the worlds inferior to man, it is not right and good when applied to the human world, and can never give unity to our social life. For Selfishness in the social world is not a uniting, but dividing term. The men who are united only by the bond of a common selfish interest are not united at all. Or they are united only as the European nations to-day are united in a peace, which can only be maintained by large and threatening standing armies in every one of those nations, and which at any moment may be sharply broken, when any nation feels that it is strong enough to break it; then all the nations will be at each other's throats again. The ultimate tendency of the principle of Selfishness is not to unite men more and more, but to crush and overcome them, to weed them out, to eliminate them, and more and more destroy them, until at last— this is its ultimate tendency—until at last only one strongest man survives.

Not by the principle of Selfishness, or self-interest, however enlightened, can the social world be united; and the union which it gives, or the peace which it gives is an armed peace, which, Selfishness having made, Selfishness can break. Neither can that union be found, in commerce or in trade, as you men of business should know, although some persons to-day are trying hard to find it in that manner, thinking that if they can only increase and multiply the industrial opportunities and commercial and trading facilities of the world, and make the world more prosperous, that then they will gather the world together and make the world one. That, too, is a union which, in its last analysis, rests on Selfishness, and is therefore not a lasting union, is not a true union, is not a union at all. For while men in business and trade seem to be united, they are in fact very often divided, or they are united only as long as it is to their interest to be united, and then no longer united. Everybody in business is avowedly there for himself, helping others if he can, but not if it hurts himself; and the union thus effected is a brittle union, and it may crack, as very often it does crack, as here and there it is cracking in our social life to-day, with great protentous lines of threatening cleavage in it.

Not by the selfish struggle for existence can the social life be united. Yet in some way it must be united. The human heart demands it; the human mind demands it; the best modern thought demands it; the sense of economy, making against waste, demands it. All other things have been gathered up into one. How shall the social life be gathered up into one? Not by Selfishness, no matter what euphemistic synonym we interchange it with, but by Righteousness. Yes, but what is Righteousness? According to Jesus Christ Righteousness is just the opposite of Selfishness. Selfishness is the die upon which Righteousness is stamped; and just as between the die and the image stamped upon it we find what may be called "opposite resemblances," so does Righteousness answer to Selfishness by what may be called "opposite resemblances." Patient, strong, brave, diligent, industrious, getting on in life, in the one case for yourself, only for yourself. Then patient, brave, diligent, strong, rich, getting on in life, not only for yourself but for your neighbor too, your neighbor *as* yourself. That, says Christ, is Righteousness. That is the righteous life; that is the righteous man. Not merely the man who is trying, however honestly or fairly or uprightly, simply to push himself along, but the man who is also trying to push his neighbor along; cultivated, educated, strong, not only for himself but for his neighbor too, pushing *him* along. That, says Christ, is Righteousness. That is a righteous man; that is a right man, the way in which a man was made and meant to live; thus drawing others to him, carying others with him, taking them along as he takes himself along, and more and more as he is lifted up, so more and more lifting others up; all of them together gathered into one.

That is the law. Yes, the law, ordained of God for human life on earth, which to human life on earth its unity can give. That is the law which in Jesus Christ we see, not only by Him taught, but also by Him lived, and in the observance of which this world will become a Christian world at last, and all things in it be gathered up into Jesus Christ. And so it is now becoming a Christian world. There is I know division in it, and strife, and tumult, and discord. Alas, I know it well; we all know it well. Political strife, national strife, social strife, theological strife, ecclesiastical strife; and yet now as never before in the history of mankind do we see and find a human love and sympathy and ministration in it, with an earnestness never so earnest, with a self-sacrificingness never so self-sacrificing, with a bountifulness never so bountiful, with a service never so helpful, so generous, so great, and of such far-reaching scope, shining or sounding through it all, the tumult and the strife.

May I illustrate? I remember once to have read of a bird of beautiful song which, in the course of its heavenward flight, was struck by the gathering storm; struck, but it was not silenced. And as the spreading and bulging cloud touched the edge of the sun, and the twilight gloom and darkness fell over the face of the earth, and the flash of the lightning shone, and the voice of the thunder broke, and the blast of the hurricane blew, and the wind came out of its prison house, and the tempest bowed the trees, in it all, above it all, somehow singing through it all, the long-resounding silvery note of the beautiful song was heard, and which survived the storm. So through all the battling strifes of battling creeds and arms, the tumult and the crash, the moral and mental confusion, the theological bewilderment, the ecclesiastical estrangement; yes; in and through it all, the long-resounding note, vibrating through the ages, yet coming out to-day with an accent never so clear,—" Your neighbor as yourself: your neighbor as yourself"; the long-resounding note of the great triumphant song of Jesus Christ is heard!

Look at the Christian Church to-day. What is it doing? Not putting forward now so much, though still of course maintaining its doctrines and its creeds; yet now as never before reaching out its helping hand to the human life about it, and with all the strength it possesses, trying to gather up that human life about it and to make it one. Through all the divisions, the discords and the strifes, the long-resounding note of Jesus Christ is heard,—" Your neighbor as yourself."

Look at the nation to-day. What is the Nation doing? Engaging in a struggle and going to a conflict which some tried in vain to avert, but which, having come, we must all support, and can; chiefly because in all that dark and stormful sky, that lowering thunder gloom, that vivid lightning flash, in all that storm and darkness this singular note is heard, scarcely indeed if ever heard in any war before,—" Your neighbor as yourself: your neighbor as yourself!"

And so, my friends, if you look beneath the surface of things, if you penetrate to the heart of the storms and strifes, you there may find the signs of the coming triumph and ascendency of Jesus Christ; not perhaps of the theological Christ, or the ecclesiastical Christ, as you and I regard Him, but the Divine Christ, with His Divine message and mission for the world—" Your neighbor as yourself!"

And more and more throughout the world, spreading, growing, singing, that keynote will be heard. More and more throughout the world that righteousness will be seen, inspiring the world, redeeming the world, contributing more and more to the unity of the world, with all things in it at last gathered up into Jesus Christ!

THE FULFILLING VISION.

These things saith the Amen, the faithful and true witness, the beginning of the creation of God.—
REVELATION iii. 14.

THE FULFILLING VISION.

This word "Amen" means as you know verification, ratification. In that sense we use it at the end of a prayer or a Creed, to ratify the prayer or the Creed, to signify thus in a word that that is what we believe, what we have just recited, what we have just repeated; that that is what we believe. Using it however in that connection and sense, we use it as a kind of interjected adverb. In the text it is used as a noun, as the name or title of Christ, Who is thus described or portrayed, as the Person in Whom we find the embodiment of what we believe, the fulfilment of what we believe, the consummating finale, the *Amen* of what we believe.

Let us make that our subject: Jesus Christ as the Amen of Faith.

First of all, however, I must occupy your attention for a few moments in trying to explain what I mean by "faith" or what I think the Christian religion means. The impression is sometimes made, even when it is not sought to be made, that faith is opposed to reason, or reason opposed to faith; and that if we desire faith, reason will have to go. Now, if that be the case, that faith is opposed to reason, then it is not reason that will have to go; it is *faith* that will have to go; for whenever an issue with reason is made, reason will always, ultimately, win. But that is not the case. Faith is *not* opposed to reason. It is through the exercise of reason, or of reasonableness, that we reach faith.

Suppose, for instance, we should be told that we must believe what the Bible says, or the Church says, or the Pope says. We must first somehow be persuaded and convinced that it is reasonable to believe what the Bible says, or what the Church says, or what the Pope says. How otherwise can we, as reasonable creatures, believe it? Faith in that case is not faith; it is ignorance, credulity, superstition. But, no; the antithesis of faith is not reason, the antithesis of faith is sight; and the contention of one who is contending for faith is not with the man who says "I will believe only what is reasonable"; that is right, always right; his contention is with the man who says "I will believe only what I can *see*"; that is *not* right. The man who believes only what he can see is not a right man; or, using a more familiar and common term, he is not a righteous man; and, if it be not reasonable not to be righteous, he is not a reasonable man.

But is it true that the man who believes only what he can see is not a righteous man? Surely it is. What is it to be a righteous man? It is, to say the least, to be an honest man. What is it to be an honest man? Who is the honest man? Is it the man who is honest simply because he sees that honesty, as we commonly say, is the "best policy"? No; for sometimes it is not just exactly the best policy; and a little departure from honesty, a little meandering and prevaricating moral crookedness, not too much, but a little, carefully concealed and ambushed, and artfully and ingeniously practised, so as not to be found out, is the "best policy" to pursue, so far as the attainment of some temporal end is concerned! If that be the case, then what becomes of his honesty? It is gone. That is its logical and final Amen—vanishment, disappearance, nothing. And the man who is honest simply because he sees that honesty is as a rule the best policy to pursue, is not an honest man, is not a righteous man!

So with the other elements and attributes of righteousness; virtuousness, truthfulness, pureness, probity, courage, honor; sometimes they pay in worldly coin and advantage, usually they pay; but sometimes they do not. And the best way at times of

getting on, with a temporal getting on—as some of
the managing editors of some of our daily papers
are keen enough to see—is to be *not* truthful, and
not virtuous, and *not* pure; not in their personal
and domestic relations, perhaps, but as managing
editors. If one is to believe only what he sees, then
that is what he sees, and that is what he is; that is
the end, the Amen, of his righteous manhood. Or,
as Falstaff puts it, when contemplating the possibility of being seriously hurt in some fight in which
he is about to engage, " Well, no matter," he says,
" honor pricks me on. But what if honor prick me
off when I come on? How then? Can honor set
a leg? No. Or an arm? No. Or take away the
grief of a wound? No. Honor hath no skill in
surgery, then? No. What is Honor? A word.
What is in that word " Honor"? Air. Who hath it?
He that died a Wednesday. Doth he hear it? No.
Doth he feel it? No. Is it insensible? Yea, to the
dead. But will it not live with the living? No.
Why? Detraction will not suffer it; therefore I'll
none of it. Honor's a mere 'scutcheon. And so
ends my catechism."

And so, logically, ends every catechism and every
decalogue, and every moral code, based upon the
theory that it is reasonable to believe only what

we see. That is its Amen—vanishment, disappearance; nothing!

If, then, righteousness be reasonable, and if to live by what we see does not make for righteousness, but against it, then to live by what we see is not a reasonable way to live. It is reasonable to live in some other way. That is what faith says. That is what faith is, that principle in us, that quality, that instinct—call it what you please, but it is in us—which predicates and asserts the existence in the universe of a moral government about us, unseen, unseeable, but real; whose moral laws pervade it, and will ultimately rule and control it, which makes us feel that we *ought*, though the whole of the physical universe with all of its physical forms and all its physical forces should vanish and cease to be; which makes us feel that we *ought*—sublimest word and greatest which human speech can frame—that we *ought* to obey those laws. That is faith in its essence, the testimony given by the moral nature of man to the existence in the universe of a moral government about him. That is faith. That is what makes him in fact a moral man, a *right* man, a righteous man; faith—not in what he sees, but in what he does not see and cannot, which makes him at times go against what he sees, his temporal ease and peace and comfort and prosperity and temporal reward; which makes him on the earth a right, a righteous man!

That is the righteousness which in the Bible we find, which there in so many persons so brightly shines; and who are there described at times as wandering about the earth, in deserts, dens, caves, with trials of cruel mockings, scourgings, woundings, hurtings, dyings; tormented, tempted, tortured, not accepting deliverance, who, through faith, wrought righteousness on the earth! That is the righteousness which out of the Bible we find, the righteousness that exalts the individual, that exalts the nation, that exalts the world at large; the righteousness which, through faith, in the world at large is wrought!

What is the end of it—that righteousness through faith—what is the consummation of it? Will it also perish and disappear, and cease in time to be, that highest form of living, that noblest form of living, that living now by faith, imparting to our living now its highest, noblest worth: will it also die: is that the end of it? Is that its Amen, to be said at last, or sung, or heard in requiem above it? Every moral instinct in the nature of man declares what the Bible itself declares, that somewhere in the universe—we see and know not where—there is a Jesus Christ; that the righteousness which through faith is wrought, to a Jesus Christ it points; that the righteousness which through faith is wrought, to a Jesus Christ it goes; that somewhere in the universe to a Jesus Christ it leads, the embodiment there of faith, the fulfilment there of faith, the consummating finale, the great Amen, of faith!

Given the existence of a moral nature in man, and given the existence of a moral government in the universe, and the existence of a Jesus Christ somewhere in the universe, as the ultimate consummation of that moral nature and that moral government, becomes a moral necessity. If Jesus Christ did not in fact exist, man's moral nature would invent him. But He *does* exist, has existed, will exist, the beginning of the moral creation of God, the end of the moral creation of God; sounding in triumphant tones at last through the whole of the moral creation of God, as its great and glad Amen. Not yet indeed do we hear it, that great Amen, of the righteousness wrought by faith; not yet indeed do we hear it, the time has not yet come. We are now in the midst of the prayer; we are now in the midst of the Creed, or we are now in the midst of the Liturgy of the righteousness wrought by faith, repeating it, reciting, trying now to live it, finding now at times that it is so hard to live, tempted now at times not to continue to live it, with falls and lapses from it, and haltings and stumblings in it, yet getting up again and going on, and trying still to say it, to do it, and to be it! We are now in the midst of it; we have not reached the end of it, but we are on the way to reach it! We are on the way to find it, in Jesus Christ to reach it, to find it, to see it, to know it, in Jesus Christ to hear it!

Is it to be so, that we shall at last reach that great Amen of faith? Then, let us go on, and work, and suffer, and not weary, and continue by faith to live! Is it to be so, that we shall at last hear it, that great Amen of faith, whose echoes now we faintly hear sounding in our hearts? Then, let us wait, in hope and patience wait, and continue by faith to live! Is it to be so? Then is the way of faith on earth both reasonable and right. And rough and hard and dark though it be at times yet as it is, so be it, God help us, till the end come; and gathered up into Jesus Christ, we shall say at last "Amen!"

www.ingramcontent.com/pod-product-compliance
Lightning Source LLC
Chambersburg PA
CBHW031929230426
43672CB00010B/1862